Misconceptions and Simple Truths
in
Dressage

H. L. M. van Schaik

Misconceptions and Simple Truths in Dressage

J. A. Allen
London

British Library Cataloguing in Publication Data

Van Schaik, H. L. M., *1899–*
  Misconceptions and simple truths in dressage. –
  2nd ed.
  1. Dressage
  I. Title
  636.1'0886

ISBN 0–85131–489–9

First edition 1986

Second edition 1989

First published in Great Britain by
J. A. Allen & Company Limited,
1, Lower Grosvenor Place, Buckingham Palace Road,
London SW1W 0EL

Book production Bill Ireson
Filmset by Fakenham Photosetting Ltd, Fakenham, Norfolk
Printed by St Edmundsbury Press, Bury St Edmunds, Suffolk

Contents

Geleitwort

Was hier dem Leser angeboten wird, ist ein auf wohlfundiertem Wissen ruhender, mit vielen gezielten Hinweisen auf die Schwachstellen gespickter Zusammenschnitt der "klassischen Grundgesetze" der Reitkunst. In allen Epochen hat ihre Beachtung Kunstwerke entstehen lassen, die zwar nie ein Menschen- und manchmal nur ein Pferdeleben zu überdauern vermochten, die aber trotzdem einen festen Platz in der Geschichte der Reitkunst behalten haben.

Der Verfasser ist ein glühender Anhänger dieser Kunst, und daher geht es ihm bei seinen Aussagen in erster Linie darum, auf die hohen Werte hinzuweisen, die in dieser Kunst beheimatet sind. Sie zählt zu jenen Künsten, die ihre Impulse nicht von der ungeheuren Motorik unserer schnellebigen Zeit empfängt, sondern im Gegenteil den Menschen eher zwingen sollte, mit Rücksicht auf seinen Partner Pferd das Tempo jenen von letzteren diktierten Gesetzen anzupassen.

Wie mir scheint, will hier der Verfasser aber nicht anklagen, sondern mit seinen Aussagen nur aufzeigen, um wieviel Schönes und Erhabenes sich sowohl der Reiter selbst bringt aber natürlich auch jener erwartungsvolle Betrachter gebracht wird, wenn die gemeinsame Leistung nicht mehr von der Harmonie des Zusammenspiels, sondern nur noch vom ergeizigen Denken des Menschen diktiert wird. Es gehen damit nicht nur die der Kunst als wichtige Basis dienenden Grundsätze verloren, sondern mehr und mehr wird sie für den Außenstehenden uninteressant und damit geht langsam aber auch ihre Anziehungskraft, die sie eh und je hatte, verloren.

Wenn diese Schrift auch in erster Linie für den Fachmann bestimmt ist und einen oder den anderen von ihnen zum Nachdenken bewegen soll, wird sie auch den nur am Rande an der Materie Interessierten etwas zu sagen und gerade letzterem den Blick für die Unterschiede zu schärfen vermögen. Um echte Reitkunst von reiner Erfolgshysterie unterscheiden zu können, bedarf es viel weninger eines großen Fachwissens, als der Bereitschaft, die Komponenten dieser Kunst auf sich wirken zu lassen.

Es sei daher dem Verfasser für diesen Dienst ehrlich gedankt. Seine Aussagen haben umso mehr Gewicht, als sie auf persönlich Erlebtem und Erarbeitetem beruhen und daher mit hoher Uberzeugungskraft ausgestattet sind.

BRIGADIER-GENERAL KURT ALBRECHT

Foreword (translation)

Here the reader is offered a poignant cross-section of the "classical principles" of the art of riding, based on a very sound background of knowledge. This perspective is established through the use of many telling examples of the art's weaknesses. In every era works of art were created through acknowledgement of the art. These works of art never lived longer than a human life, sometimes not longer than one horse's life. Nevertheless, they have held a secure place in the history of the art of riding.

The author is a fervent fan of this art, and therefore his main purpose is to emphasise the high values that are within this art. Classical riding should be one of those arts unaffected by the monstrous drive of today's fast pace. In fact, this art should force us to choose a tempo that fits the high standards for consideration of our partner, the horse.

It appears to me that the author is not accusing with his comments, but rather pointing out how much beauty for both rider and hopeful spectator is lost when man's ambitious drive dictates what should transpire between horse and rider rather than letting the harmony in the combined effort of the two parties be the guide. Ironically, not only do the classical principles get lost with this ambitious drive but also the interest and fascination of the spectators.

Although this book is perhaps speaking more directly to the professional and may move one or the other to ponder, it will also appeal to those only marginally interested and will sharpen their ability to see the differences mentioned. It takes much less riding expertise to see the difference between real art in riding and pure ambition than it takes readiness to let the components of the art touch you through your senses.

I honestly thank the author for this service. His statements carry that much more weight and conviction because they are based on personal experience.

BRIGADIER-GENERAL KURT ALBRECHT, *former Director of the Spanish Riding School*

Acknowledgements

This book would never have been embarked upon without the help of many people.

Through the provocation of Jean-Marc Oppenheim I began this endeavour. He brought order to the chaos of articles I had written for different publications over the years and persuaded me to make a book out of them.

Stephanie Grant took the next step and made the tentative layout of the book by organising the different articles in chapters. She made several very valuable suggestions in the preparatory stages. Frances O'Reilly did the final editing and also aided me in the completion stages of the text with her valuable suggestions and her expertise. Carol Selikowitz did all the technical photographs, not only by pressing the button on her camera but also by making the decisions on how she wanted them taken. Her talent included the reproductions of some of my older photographs and all of the processing. Sheila McLevedge, my assistant since 1974, posed for the pictures, did the artwork for the line drawings and has been a patient listener and sharp critic when I rambled on about my ideas. Walter Carrington and Daniel Pevsner introduced me to the Alexander Technique and made me understand the importance of the use of the abdominal muscles in order to acquire a functional and elegant position on the horse.

I feel very indebted to all these good friends.

That Brigadier-General Kurt Albrecht, former Director of the Spanish Riding School, was willing to write the Foreword is a great honour, for which I feel very grateful. My thanks also to Cindy Sydnor for her translation.

List of Illustrations

It is not necessary to have expectations in order to start something, neither to be successful in order to persevere

WILLIAM OF ORANGE

Introduction to the First Edition

Unity in the movement of man and horse is the goal of equitation, the art of riding. Without this unity no movements in high collection are possible, and this unity is only possible when there is a mutual confidence between man and horse. For those who are bewildered by all of the complicated theories and the contradictory methods in achieving such unity, I have in this book tried to focus on a few basic truths which, when really understood, will help dissolve misconceptions and show the way to classical equitation and also to the modern concept of riding. Whenever man confronts the horse, he should try to inspire confidence. This begins when handling the young animal, continues while schooling, and later while using the horse for work. Therefore, take your time: don't hurt the horse by being brusque, don't fall in the saddle when mounting, and don't yank in the reins. Don't forget the horse has to adapt himself to the task of carrying the rider. With a young horse, allow the muscles to develop, the bones to grow, and the tendons and ligaments to become strong.

I won't go into detail because there are many excellent books describing the handling and the schooling of the young horse. The reason that I mention these things is that there are also books written advocating a quick and easy way. There is no such thing as a quick and easy way in equitation. Physical development takes time, and all through history the great masters of equitation have been concerned with schooling the horse in such a way that he is able to carry a rider with the least wear for himself and the most comfort for the rider, while developing the horses' muscles in such a way that he is physically able to be obedient in executing the movements required. The horse needs a lot of gymnastic exercise to enable him to redistribute his weight, without which no movements in equitation are possible. When we ask movements of a horse which he cannot make because his muscles are not yet developed, we not only ruin him physically but also mentally.

In the early 1960s, I started writing, off and on, articles about certain aspects of the movements asked for in dressage tests. I enjoy judging, but especially at the lower levels it gives me a feeling of frustration. Most of the people riding in those tests try very hard and do their utmost, but most of the time it is all wrong, because they don't really know what they are supposed to do. It is impossible, considering the time and space, to explain in the commentary on the score sheet why so many things are wrong, and what should be done to correct them, so in my articles I tried to explain several of the problems. The first part of this book deals with special problems and is based on those articles, though they have been rewritten, expanded and enlarged; new problems have been dealt with as well.

The Reflections (Chapter 14) are based on articles I wrote after attending international dressage shows. The first article was written after I had watched the European Dressage Championships in Wolfsburg in 1969. I was very disappointed, and the more I travelled and the more I saw, the more my concern for the future of classical dressage grew. Erich Glahn had warned in 1956 against the dangers that were threatening classical equitation. In 1974 Miss Oehlert, a pupil of Egon von Neindorff, asked in an article in the German magazine *Sankt Georg* if the art of riding should be sacrificed to dressage sport. I always had hoped that people more qualified than I and more able to express their thoughts would come to the fore to defend classical equitation, but nobody did. There are an increasing number of people who sense that there is something wrong with the way dressage is going. Those people gave me the inspiration to continue to write and to try to find out what is really wrong with the modern interpretation of classical equitation. I hoped eventually to find the ways to correct the wrongs as a result of my reflections after the 1984 Olympic Games in Los Angeles. I have come up with a series of possible solutions that may save classical equitation, and these are gathered at the end of the Reflections.

Introduction to the Second Edition

I am very grateful to Mr. J. A. Allen and Mrs. Caroline Burt, Editorial Manager, for allowing me to make important revisions and add new chapters to this second edition of *Misconceptions and Simple Truths in Dressage*.

The final date of the manuscript of the first edition was 1985. Since then my perception of different problems encountered in the way classical equitation is being practised, in this day and age, has deepened my understanding of phenomena that I previously described as mysteries so that they are not mysteries any more, thanks to the information from experts.

An intense study of the Duke of Newcastle's *Méthode Nouvelle* has made me understand that la Guérinière was the real inventor of the shoulder-in but that Newcastle had paved the way for la Guérinière, while he too was looking for a way to loosen the shoulders but stayed on the wrong track.

The new chapters consist of articles I wrote in connection with developments that bothered me in present day equitation.

I thank Pepper Mainwaring Healey for finding concise expressions for me and for smoothing my sometimes awkward phrasing.

Cavendish, Vermont 1988.

Elegance on horseback consists of a straight and free position as a result of a well balanced body; as a result the rider maintains, during all the movements the horse makes, without losing his seat, as much as he is able to, in an appropriate balance, an air of comfort and freedom, which makes him an elegant rider

LA GUÉRINIÈRE

1 The Rider's Position

When Louis XIII began his riding lessons with Antoine de Pluvinel, the first thing he asked was, "What do you expect first of your pupil?" De Pluvinel answered, "That he be an elegant rider." ("Qu'il soit bel homme de cheval.") The King then asked, "What distinction do you make between an elegant rider and a good rider (bon homme de cheval)?" To this de Pluvinel answered, "I make a great distinction because it would be very embarrassing to be a good rider without being an elegant rider. It is however, possible to be an elegant rider without being a good rider." This conversation took place during the 16th century when, of course, nobody had ever heard of dressage competitions. Unfortunately, today it is a fact that elegant riders are seen rarely, and that good riders are not at all embarrassed by the fact that they are very often not elegant riders. This is a pity, because I am convinced that the functionally correct position is an elegant position.

A very important part of the rider's position is his seat. The rider may have a very elegant position, but if his seat is not functional, then the elegant position is worthless. That is the reason de Pluvinel made the distinction between "the elegant rider" and "the good rider".

As I see it, the seat has to have three qualities to be functional: it has to be secure; it has to be light and immobile; it should be able to act as an aid.

First, the only way to be secure on a horse is to be in balance. All muscular efforts made to stay on the horse cause rigidities and make it impossible for the rider to give the correct aid and to feel the horse.

One of the principal parts of the human being is the spinal column, because by balancing it forward and backward, one can influence the centre of gravity. It is evident that the rider can do this only if he prevents his back from collapsing, which happens if he lets go with his abdominal muscles.

Second, the rider should do his utmost to be light on the horse and try to avoid all unnecessary movements. It is evident that the less of a burden the rider is for the horse, the better and the longer the horse will be able to serve his rider. The only way a rider can make himself light on a horse and avoid unnecessary movements is to make himself tall by using the abdominal muscles. This will prevent him from sitting like a sack of grain on the horse.

There is a widespread misconception about the deep seat: it does not mean that the rider should press his seat into the saddle, it does mean that he should not tighten the muscles in his seat to such an extent that it becomes rigid and puts him on top of the saddle. The seat becomes deep when he decontracts his seat muscles so that all of his seat is in contact with the saddle.

It is also evident that the rider should not, during the sitting trot, bounce in the saddle. The rider should only attempt to sit a horse that has had so much schooling that he is able to use his back; on a horse that is unable to do this the rider should only rise to the trot.

I never really understood why the stretching of the spine would eliminate the bouncing. I think that I have found the answer to this question in *Plaisirs Equestres No. 155*, in an article written by Louis Fabre. This author claims that because of the cushioning potential of the discs between the vertebrae, the shocks will fade away, vertebra after vertebra, during the stretching of the spine. I have the verdict of one medical doctor who thinks that there is a strong possibility that this thesis is correct.

Third, the seat should be able to act as an aid. The book *Das Gymnasium des Reiters* by H. and V. Schusdziarra (a father–son combination; both are M.D.s) has taught me that the back part of the seatbones pressing in the saddle, or, for that matter, on the horse's back, is what has an impulse-creating influence. By using his abdominal muscles, the rider can tilt his pelvis forward and upward, which makes the seatbones, where they are widest apart, push into the saddle.

Why this pressing of the seatbones creates impulsion has been a mystery to me. Recently I learned from Nancy Nicholson, Ph.D., who has an extensive knowledge of the horse's muscles, thanks to the influence of Jack Meagher, that there is indeed a sensitive spot not too far from the withers. As I understand it, there is a nexus of numerous muscles connected to the trunk of the thorax

22

and to the scapula. There is also an acupuncture spot in the same region.

I shall now try to explain how this elegant, functional position can be achieved. The reader will have noticed that in order to achieve all three requisites, I have stressed the necessity to use the abdominal muscles. In other words, one can only stretch the spine by using the abdominal muscles. The teachings of the Alexander Technique have confirmed in me the conviction that only by making oneself tall and by using the abdominal muscles, can one be secure, light and still on a horse and able to create impulsion. In other words, one can only stretch the spine by using the abdominal muscles.

It is commonly accepted that the rider should sit straight, that there should be one line from shoulders to seat-bones to heels, and that he should be plumb on his seat-bones. Here is where the difficulties start. Sitting straight on a chair and sitting straight on a horse are two totally different positions. When we sit upright on a chair, we sit on the foremost part of the seat-bones, and when we stretch to be straight we hollow the lumbar part of the spine. On a horse, we should sit on the back part of the seat-bones.

If the rider sits on a horse the way he sits on a chair, his knees will be too high; he will sit partly on his thighs; and the upper body will be behind the vertical line of shoulders to seat-bones to heels. He will also sit too close to the cantle; thus the centre of gravity is not aligned with the horse's centre of gravity. All this results in the rider not being able to influence the horse properly.

It is difficult to achieve the correct position, and it is difficult to explain it. In no other walk of life do we have to adopt a position which takes our shoulders and heels back and tilts our pelvis forward and upward. A French author, as a consequence, once said: "Man was not created to ride horseback."

When one tries to sit straight, the emphasis should be put on the functioning of the abdominal muscles and *not* on the back. The advantage of using the abdominal muscles is that it prevents "belly dancing" (the constant back and forth motion of the pelvis) and also bobbing of the head. It also prevents the small of the back from becoming hollow, and in addition, it increases the tone of the leg muscles. There was a time when a straight back meant a hollow

23

back. A hollow back is functionally incorrect, because it causes internal stress as well as rigidity. There are many people who believe that belly dancing is proof of suppleness. This is a misconception, because this movement is only possible when the abdominal muscles are not engaged. When used correctly, the abdominal muscles are responsible for the independent and balanced seat that we believe is the most influential on the horse and also the most elegant. They are not only a powerful help to, but also a discreet way of, creating impulsion. Belly dancing in the saddle is not only functionally incorrect, but is also unaesthetic.

In order to prevent the rider from sitting on the end of his spine, thereby curving the small of the back, the angle of the hip-joint has to be widened and the knees have to be pushed down. There should be a little bend in the knee-joint; in this way it is not difficult to achieve the line; shoulders, seat-bones, heels. The rider should be very careful not to bring the knees too deep, as this will put him on the front part of the seat-bones, even on the pubic bone. In order to prevent the knees from being too straight, the rider should make sure that the lumbar part of his spine is upright and that the lower legs are not too far back.

The elegant rider who sits correctly should have his head up; he should look over the world. When the chin drops, the head follows and the spine collapses. The Alexander Technique taught me that the head has to be balanced; in other words, the rider should not use his neck muscles. Using those muscles to keep the chin up creates tension and gives the appearance of a "bull neck". On a horse one should avoid any kind of rigidity; correct riding entails the rider reacting to what he is feeling, and being rigid makes feeling what is going on with the horse impossible. Therefore, balance your head; do not force it up.

The elbows should be slightly bent. This, with free shoulders will guarantee an elasic contact with the horse's mouth. Elasticity is impossible with stretched elbows and a narrow chest. There should be a straight, horizontal line from the elbows, through the hands, to the horse's mouth. If the hands are below this line, pressure will be put on the bars of the horse's mouth, and the head will go up. If the hands come above that line, the horse will come behind the bit.

The rider should never use his biceps. If he does, he will lock the elbow joint, resulting in a dead hand. When the rider wants to resist he should take a deep breath, widening his chest which will help in using the back muscles and the triceps. In this way the rider will elastically increase the tension in the reins. He should never pull. Neither should the rider squeeze with his thighs. If he does, he can not use his lower legs, which he has to use in order to give the aids correctly. His lower legs should, as Seunig once put it, stick like wet towels to the horse's barrel. In this way they are always in place, ready to be used. The rider should pull his toes up and have light contact with the stirrup irons. If the heels are pushed down too much the lower leg will tend to go too far forward. In case a rider has the tendency to ride with the legs too far back, then the correction is to push the heels down. Knee-joints and ankle-joints should never be locked. They are shock absorbers; if they are locked, they cannot function as such.

When a rider has to mount a young or unschooled horse for the first time, mount a horse with a cold back or ride over cavaletti, it is advisable to keep his seat-bones out of the saddle by putting his bodyweight on his thighs and on the stirrup irons. The rider brings his body slightly forward, being sure to use his abdominal muscles, in order to prevent his spine from collapsing and consequently losing his balance.

There are many people, teachers and riders, who firmly believe in the usefulness of a three-point seat. I think that there are two different interpretations of the phrase *three-point seat*. One is "the two seat bones and the pubic bone" touching the saddle and the other one is "the two seat bones and the coccyx" touching the saddle. In *Das Gymnasium des Reiters*, the verdict about the first interpretation is short: "anatomically impossible". The second version is seldom mentioned because it is the result of "bracing the backbone".

The expression "bracing the backbone" was introduced into dressage vernacular by an incorrect translation of an expression that Müeseler used in his book *Reitlehre*: "das Kreuz anspannen"; literally translated "to tighten the small of the back". A picture in Müeseler's book shows an arrow pointing to the small of the back. The backbone is the whole spinal column, the small of the back is a part of it. The text explains that because of such tightening, the sacrum is being pushed forward. Since the sacrum is the junction between spine and pelvis, the pelvis rotates in such a way that the back part goes down and the front part goes up. A second arrow points downward and could have influenced the translator in thinking that the sacrum was supposed to do the pushing, resulting in getting the coccyx involved.

It has always been my understanding that bracing, as the dictionary describes it, means imparting rigidity. This is, of course, a concept that has no place in classical equitation.

Müeseler realizes the importance of the back part of the seatbones but, perhaps unintentionally, gets the sacrum involved. Clearly he does not recognize the importance of the abdominal muscles. This and the incorrect translation has caused a lot of misconceptions.

To recapitulate: if you want to be a good and elegant rider, use your abdominal muscles, making yourself tall. This will make you a functional rider because it will help you create impulsion and it will make you an elegant rider, who is in control of his body, free of rigidities and looking over the world.

The principle lies in collaboration. Quiet, subtle constraint gives way to gentle marital servitude, which implies a conquest, properly progressive of the body and the soul of the spouse. And upon achievement of this intimacy the rider succeeds in making himself understood by touches, signs and brainwaves

SOBÈNE OLSTEF

2 Natural Reactions

One of the reasons why learning to ride is so difficult is that the natural reactions can be dangerous, or at least counterproductive when one is riding a horse. Being frightened by something unexpected causes one to cringe, perhaps a remnant from times when we lived in the wilderness and our first reaction to being threatened was to make ourselves small. On a horse, this reaction is the surest way of being deposed.

When a horse moves off, the rider's natural reaction is to hang on to the reins, to lean forward with the knees and the heels up, with the result that the horse wants to go even faster. The rider's trained reaction should be to relax the seat and leg muscles, retain an upright position and give with the hands. An example of the effectiveness of giving is: when a jockey on the flat wants to slow down, he gives with his hands and when he wants to go faster he takes hold of the reins. Remaining in an upright position prevents the rider falling forward and over the horse's neck or just from falling off. The relaxation of the seat and leg muscles calms the horse by removing a cause of tension.

To turn a horse a rider will naturally pull his rein in the direction he wants to go towards his body and yield with the outside rein. I call this technique "riding the bicycle". If you do this there is a very good chance that, should the horse not want to go in the direction you want him to, he will throw himself on the outside shoulder and move off in the opposite direction.

If, for example, the horse does not want to go to the left, he will throw himself on the right shoulder, taking the opportunity offered by the rider who is hanging on the left rein. A very common example of this situation occurs in an indoor arena when a horse becomes frightened of noises or a shadow on the wall and tries to get off the wall by throwing himself over the inside shoulder. Most riders will pull on the outside rein to try to keep the horse on the wall. Because the rider pulls the horse's head to the outside, to the wall, bending to face the outside, he helps the horse to move to the inside of the arena. What the rider should do in a case like this, as soon as he feels that there is going to be trouble, is to close the inside leg on the girth, which often gives confidence to the horse. The inner leg in this situation should never be put behind the girth, because this would push the hindquarters to the outside, thus helping the horse to go over the inside shoulder.

If the rider feels that the horse is really upset, he should close his inside leg and, at the same time, he should bring his inside arm up as high as possible with a stretched elbow, pressing the inner rein against the horse's neck as a kind of a barrier. The outside rein should have about the same tension as the inside rein, so that it can function as a counterweight. This will prevent the horse from going over the inside shoulder, because in this way the rider bends the horse around his inside leg. The high hand tilts the lower part of the head sideways and upward, which has an effect on the last two vertebrae of the horse's neck (atlas axis). The elbow has to be stretched because the more the force applied goes up, and not backwards towards the rider's body, the less interference there will be with the forward movement. In a situation like this, it is vital that the horse keeps moving. In case the rider has been too late with the leg and the high hand, and the horse is already over the shoulder, away from the wall, the rider has to try to make a circle to the inside. The best way to do this is to use opening rein, making the horse bend around the rider's inside leg. The rider should keep the horse on the circle until the horse surrenders and bends. Then the rider should take the horse back to the wall, the inside hand high and maintaining the bend; this is a kind of rough, pragmatic shoulder-in; the horse should not be allowed to look to the outside. By applying this technique the rider has put the horse on the aids and has created a barrier to prevent the horse from moving away from the spot he is afraid of.

It is of course true that one should let the horse look at what frightens him. But it is a misconception that one can do this by pulling on the rein on the side of the frightening object. When one wants to show the horse the object of his fears, then go at it in a straight line and keep the horse straight by enclosing the neck between the reins. If possible, begin to walk in a straight line towards the object from a point approximately three horse-lengths away. Make frequent halts and caress the horse, making sure that he stays straight. The closer the object, the longer the halts and the petting should last. Allow the horse to sniff at what scared him. Once there, he very likely will have no further interest.

It is of the utmost importance that the rider changes his natural reactions, adapting them to the new situation of sitting on a horse. Only when the rider has trained his reactions will he be able to develop an independent seat. This will enable him to use the aids correctly, in an elastic and feeling way, and not mechanically.

Unqualified disobedience is a frequent misconception, when the rider is not only demanding but not listening to the horse. If the horse is a strong personality the result is a notoriously resistant animal; if the horse has a submissive, weak personality, it can be brainwashed into a mechanical automat, a zombie. Both are contrary to correct dressage

TIBOR PADANYI

3 The Aids

The word "aids" derives from to aid, to help. In French the word is "les aides"; in German "die Hilfen"; in Dutch "de hulpen". Xenophon used a word with an overall meaning of "to indicate". Since I want to stress the fact that the idea of helping the horse permeates the whole literature of equitation, I need to make a short digression into history.

When man made the transition from eating the horse to using him, it was to be expected that in the beginning there was fear on both sides. Man feared the horse because he was strong and unpredictable; the horse feared man because he hurt him and tried to constrain him. I presume that once man tried to use the horse, some patient people found out that the horse is not an aggressive animal, but that he can become aggressive when constrained and treated in a cruel way. Perhaps this was the beginning of psychological insight.

By Xenophon's time (380 B C) a lot of progress had been made in achieving a more balanced relationship between man and horse, changing from antagonism to co-operation. Xenophon makes this clear: "One should never lose one's temper in treating the horse; this is the one best precept and custom in dealing with horses ... Those who compel the horse with blows make him more frightened than ever."

There were, and are to this day, frequent relapses. Federigo Grisone in his *Gli Ordini di Cavalcare* (1550), does not forget to reward and can be very gentle. However, because he believes that there are vicious horses, he can also be very cruel: he advocates hitting the horse around the ears, letting a cat, tied with its back up against a pole, crawl over the belly and between the hindlegs of the horse. When a horse does not want to move forward Grisone holds burning straw under its tail.

To this day there are still those who consider the horse to be the opponent. They claim that if the horse does not offer a fight, the rider should provoke one so that the horse knows who is the boss.

35

They do not seem to realise that if the horse wins the fight, they have lost the horse; if they win the fight, they have a mechanised, cowed horse without brilliance. In this vein we may learn something from de Pluvinel, who wrote: ". . . you must be careful not to bore him or snuff out his gentleness. Because, as with the bloom on fruit, so with horses, once it is lost it is gone forever and once the gentleness is lost one can never regain it." De Pluvinel goes on to say that when one has no consideration for one's horse, one either loses the horse's gentleness or makes him incorrectably vicious.

De Pluvinel was not the only one to understand that it makes no sense to wage battle with the horse. Long before him, Abou Bekr, master of the horse of Sultan Nacer of Egypt around 1300 said: "Schooling based on gentleness and psychology should aim at developing useful qualities by making use of the qualities the horse is born with."

Salomon de la Broue, a contemporary of de Pluvinel, wrote in *Le Cavalerice françois* (1594): "If a horse refuses or holds back this is not so much caused by malice as well as by the fear of being punished, not knowing for what cause." In the same book he wrote: "I claim that there will be disorder, resulting in a stiff back, a hard mouth and fear and sooner or later he'll become rebellious, if one tries to put his head and neck in the correct position, before the horse has learned to freely turn."

As one delves into the history of equitation, two things become clear. On the one hand a lot of progress has been made in man's attitude towards the horse and there is a lot more co–operation than antagonism. Also, techniques of how to make clear to the horse what we want him to do have been considerably refined. On the other hand, however, it is clear that either because of the mentality of some people, or through lack of understanding in how to deal with the horse, a lot of aggressive practices, such as mentioned in the above quotations, still continue. After this historical inter-mezzo, let's return to the subject, the aids.

When one looks at any group of riders, it is very clear that the gravest sins are committed with the hands. The main reasons for this are the natural reactions, mentioned in the preceding chapter. Everybody will tell you that you have to have light and elastic contact, and that you should never pull. But practically nobody has elastic contact, and most people pull. It is appalling to see how many people ride with stretched elbows, their hands halfway up the horse's neck, making it impossible for the horse to move freely and without constraint. (Especially in the beginning of a lesson one should give the horse enough room so that he can move without being constrained.) I am convinced that practically all of the problems with the horse's head are caused by bad hands. It is very difficult to decide when resisting becomes pulling. For this one has to understand the function of the arm muscles.

In books written during the heyday of military riding, one reads that the hands should be at a certain height and that the elbows should be rigid against the body. Before the First World War instruction was practically always given on schooled horses, who carried themselves. In such circumstances, a play of the fingers and a little movement of the wrist was all that was needed to guide the horse. But those horses are not available for instruction nowadays. It is very important that the rider does not constrain the horse; in other words that he does not impede the forward movement of the horse. Therefore, sitting in the functionally correct position the rider should follow, in the walk, the movement of the horse's head. He should surrender his hands to the horse, maintaining a featherlight contact with the horse's mouth. In this way the rider will get the feel of the horse's rhythm. The hands should stay in a line that includes the elbow, lower arm, hand, rein and the horse's mouth. If the hands come above that line, the horse will come behind the bit; if the hands come below that line, the head will go up. The wrist should be straight and unbroken. Only well schooled horses who have learned to carry themselves can be ridden with the wrist and the fingers.

When the rider wants to restrain the horse, he should make it more difficult for the horse to bring his head forward by tightening the elastic contact, not by using the biceps, which I call "putting on the handbrake". If the rider uses the biceps, he locks the elbow-joint, making elasticity impossible and resulting in a hand that is not able to yield. Also, the rider should never use the muscles in his lower arms. This is very important in order to avoid dancing hands in the trot. The hands have to be balanced, moved only by the horse and not by the rider's body movement. When the muscles of the lower arm are contracted, it is impossible to balance the hands. (Remember what the lower arm does when you try to balance a stick on your index finger.)

If the rider cannot use the muscles of his lower arm, nor his biceps, what does he do to restrain the horse by putting more weight on the reins? The answer is he must use his abdominal and back muscles, his triceps and pectoralis major, the muscles one uses when one expands the rib cage when taking a deep breath. It is evident that one can do this only from the independent, balanced seat.

There was a time when it was said that a rider had to use his back in order to ride correctly, in order to influence the horse in the most efficient way. This has caused a lot of misunderstanding. People thought that this meant that the rider had to lean backward in order to get the seat deeper into the saddle, that the rider had to make himself heavy. These are disastrous presumptions. How can one expect the horse to function well if the rider sits too heavily and does not align his own centre of gravity with that of the horse? The less one is a burden for the horse, the better he can serve us. Riding with the back means that by using the abdominal muscles and thereby stretching the spine one creates impulsion, and by using the back muscles in combination with the triceps one can increase and decrease the weight on the reins.

In discussing the natural reactions, I pointed to the adverse possibilities when, in making a turn, the rider pulls on the inside rein, or in other words, when he uses the direct rein of opposition. This example was the pragmatic reason never to use this rein. In schooling horses, one should be well aware of the fact that when being ridden most horses try not to use their backs. There are various theories as to why this is. It is my conviction that this stiffness is man-made. Most horses, and especially Western horses, are saddled and ridden while still quite young. Very often the young horse is taken out of the stall, has a heavy saddle thrown on his back, and then somebody is helped up whose main concern it is to stay on. There is no doubt in my mind that this is a traumatic experience for the horse. It is quite obvious that the pressure and the weight are painful because no muscles have been developed along the spine to cope with this sudden burden. In order to evade the pain, the horse tightens the muscles and a rigid back is the result. In the wild, or for that matter in pasture, one will see young unspoiled horses move with a totally decontracted body. Therefore, before putting any weight on a horse's back, first the back muscles must be developed by gymnastic exercises so that he can cope with a burden on his back. The simplest way to do this is by lungeing the horse (about which more later). Then, after a few months, gradually let the horse get used to having a weight on his back by putting a saddle on. Then lunge with the stirrups down. After a few weeks a person can hang over the saddle and a few days later can bring the right leg over to the other side and ease into the saddle, making himself as light as possible. While all this takes place, the horse should of course still be on the lunge line, the person who has regularly lunged the horse holding the line and making much of him. If, after all this, the horse still tightens his back when being ridden, one should repeat the exercises discussed above.

It is very important that a young horse learns to make correct changes of direction, because this is the way to teach him to use his back; an inexperienced rider can do a lot of harm to the horse by misusing the hands in the turns. The way to teach a totally untrained horse to change direction is to use the opening rein. The inside arm has to be stretched as far as possible to the inside, and the fingernails have to face upwards so that there is no downward pressure of the snaffle on the bars of the horse's jaw. In the beginning the outside hand should be totally passive. The action of the inside hand brings the head in, while the inside leg, with the toes up so that the calf muscle is hard, presses just behind the girth, thereby activating the inner hindleg. As soon as the horse has understood that he has to make a turn, the outside hand, a little higher than the inside, pushes the outside rein against, but never over the neck. When the outside hand goes over the neck, it will pull the head to the outside. That outside rein has to be taut enough so that it can function more or less like a stick. In this way the horse learns to move the shoulders inward on the pressure of the outside rein, the indirect rein.

When the horse does not need the help of the opening rein any more, then the time has come to teach him the correct way to make a change of direction, namely by bending round the rider's inside leg and by a slight flexing of the poll, caused by a light vibration of the rider's inside hand, so that the rider can just see the shimmer of the inside eye. A way to find out if the horse has understood the meaning of the indirect rein is to turn right, using the right opening rein, then to turn left with that same rein, now as indirect rein against the neck.

The inside rein has now to be used to get the horse to flex so that the rider can see the shimmer of the inside eye. Consequently, the horse will look in the direction he is going, and eventually he will yield to the rider's hand, by flexing the poll and letting go in the jaw.

The inside rein should be taut enough so that the vibration of the rider's hand can come through to the horse's mouth. Sometimes a gentle upward rotation of the hand is enough to get the flexion. The rider's hand should stay close to the withers, to prevent the head from coming in.

By supporting the horse with the outside rein, pressing it against the neck to ask for a change of direction, and using the inside rein only to see the shimmer of the eye, the rider will not impede the inner hindleg from making a large stride, which he would do if he pulled on that rein. The goal is to have the horse make a large stride with the inside hindleg because this effort will gymnastically develop the back muscles. Later we will discuss what the rider's legs are supposed to do during a change of direction.

The turn to the left is generally the most difficult. This is caused by the fact that most horses have a natural bend to the right side which causes the head to be carried slightly to the right. The result is that the horse takes the left rein and does not accept the right rein. There are several explanations for this phenomenon. I think that the most logical explanation is that there is no such a thing as symmetry in nature. Human beings are right and left handed; some horses take the right rein, most take the left. The result of this taking of the left rein is that, in a turn the horse will shorten the stride of the inner hindleg and will fall over the left shoulder. This should make it clear how important it is to get the horse to make a correct turn, because in this way he will be able to gymnasticise the back muscles. But how difficult this is! D'Auvergne (1729–98) wrote: "It is the never ending problem for every rider with every horse to get him to go evenly on both reins." What we ask the horse is as difficult as if we were asked to use our right and left hand in the same way.

There is a difference between the method and the goal. "Ideally the actions of the legs and the hands should be so discreet that the eye cannot catch them." (l'Hotte.) Before we can reach this goal we have to manipulate; we have to do things with the hands that are visible. This is the method. However, we should always bear in mind that the less we do, the better. Since the mouth of the horse is very sensitive, we should try never to hurt it. Hard, insensitive mouths are man-made.

In the walk the horse makes a snake-like movement from side to side; if this movement is allowed to go through to the hands, they will make a sawing movement, alternating left and right. Many horses go better when the rider carries the reins in one hand. For this reason, when riding with two hands, the rider should keep them so still and so close together that the horse has the impression that only one hand is holding the reins. The easiest way to achieve this is to put the nails and the knuckles of the thumbs together.

One has to consider what happens when the rider makes these sawing movements when he is using a curb bit. It is easy to understand that an unbroken bit makes much more movement in the horse's mouth than the snaffle when the rider has sawing hands. For this reason it is a very bad habit to carry the reins of an unbroken bit in two hands. How can the rider expect the horse to have confidence in his hands when this piece of solid metal is constantly moving in his mouth? Therefore, I believe that one should never carry the curb reins in two hands.

It is a kind of mental laziness in modern man to think that because it is easy, there is nothing wrong when one pulls right and left all the time. An example, mentioned previously, is the action of riding a bicycle when making turns.

When man first began to ride he had the reins in one hand, for the simple reason that he had only one hand available; with the other hand he carried his weapons, either for hunting or for fighting. For example, the Huns attacked without reins in their hands. They went at the enemy in waves, shooting one arrow when they were close enough; then they turned and while turning shot their second arrow; then while galloping away to make room for the next wave they shot their third arrow. To this day, the cowboy and the mounted bullfighter ride with one hand. The riders of the Spanish Riding School and a few classicists ride with a double bridle with the two curb reins in the left hand along with the left snaffle rein, and the right snaffle rein alone is in the right hand. From the basic position with hands level, the thumbs on a forty-five degree angle so that the back of the hands look like a slanting roof, the rider manipulates the reins while they are in one line: elbows, fists, mouth. When asking for a turn, the outside hand goes a little higher so that the rein presses against the neck. In transitions to a slower gait, it is often helpful to turn the nails of one hand up, and sometimes even the whole hand. The reason for this is that the snaffle, being a jointed bit, will act like a nutcracker when the rider resists with level hands, the horse's jaw will be pinched. This pinching of course hurts the horse and he will react most of the time by tossing his head up or by fighting the rider's hand.

Now I am going to focus my attention on the impulse-creating aids, the seat and the legs, which sometimes can also function as guiding aids. We have seen why it is important to have a correct position in order to apply the aids.

It is evident that the stretching of the spine can only be done by the abdominal muscles and back muscles, which makes it clear that the rider not only uses these muscles for the guiding aids but also for the impulse-creating aids. When necessary, the driving of the seat can be strengthened by the closing of the calves. When the toes are pulled up, the calf muscles harden and a lot of pressure can be applied. Under the influence of Caprilli, the slogan became "talloni bassi", the heels down. The disadvantage of pushing the heels down is that the lower leg often goes too far forward. The correct placing of the lower leg is very important; it should lie just behind the girth. For the observer the stirrup leather should be perpendicular. When the rider wants to move the haunches to the outside, the pressure should be applied a little more back. The same procedure should be applied when the rider wants to prevent the horse from bringing the haunches in or out.

Earlier we discussed making a change of direction. The focus was then on the hands. Now we will concentrate on the function of the seat and the legs while making a turn. With the inside hand the rider places the horse's head so that he sees the shimmer of the inside eye, which allows the horse to look where he is going. With the outside rein the rider pushes the horse's shoulder in the direction he wants to go. When the rider indicates with his body, by rotating the spinal column, where he wants to go, he helps the action of the outside rein. We have seen already that the pelvis can be tilted forward and upward, but the pelvis can also be rotated. Looking with the head does not influence the rider's seat, but looking or turning with the hips and shoulders does influence the rider's seat and hands.

When the rider is sitting correctly square to axis, by easing the outside rein a little he prevents it from becoming too tight, and thereby holding back. When he rotates his pelvis, bringing his outside hip-bone forward, the pressure on the inside seat-bone increases. This pressure can be reinforced by pushing the inside knee deep. It is very important that when one pushes the knee down, the heel stays in the line: shoulder, seat-bone – heel. The goal is to bend the horse around the inside leg, which is impossible if the lower leg is too far back. (The inner leg too far back is a common mistake during shoulder-in, because it pushes the haunches out and brings the horse in the position of leg-yielding, which will be discussed later in some detail (Chapter 11).)

To reinforce the pressure of the calf the rider can use spurs. The spurs should be attached to the boots in such a way that it is not necessary to pull the heels up when using them. We have already explained why the heels should never be pulled up. If a horse is lazy it may be appropriate to apply the spurs. The application should be like one stinging attack, out of the knee, without displacing the knee. One sharp attack is better than a repetition of weak ones. A contemporary French author wrote: "The spurs should be sharp as daggers so that after one application the horse knows that he has to respect them." I do not go along with this method but it is something to think about when one sees all those riders constantly poking their spurs in the horse's belly while the horse could not care less, being totally dulled to them. The purpose of the spur is to wake the horse up and to emphasise the action of the calf.

The crop should be used with totally green horses who know nothing. A little tap on the shoulder accompanied with an encouraging voice command will get the horse to move forward. Gradually this has to be accompanied by the rider stretching his spine and the closing of his calves. Generally the stretching of the spine will increase the tone in the calf muscle, which can be enough. One has to be careful not to press constantly with the calf as some horses will tighten themselves up against legs that work like a vice.

For advanced schooling, the rider should use a so-called dressage whip, rigid and 120 cm long. It should be used just behind the calf as a substitute for the spur or calf in case the horse for some reason does not react properly to the leg aids.

The best way to use the whip is to bring the hand that carries it to the inside and then to rotate the wrist. A light tap will be the result. More is generally not necessary, and often the sound against the boot is enough. One should not forget that this is an encouraging, stimulating action. By bringing the hand in and rotating the wrist one avoids yanking on the horse's mouth, which is, of course, a counterproductive action.

It should be well understood that the whip is an aid, not an instrument to punish. All too often what is called disobedience is the result of bad schooling; the horse does not understand or is physically not yet able to do what the rider asks him to do.

The rider should realise that spurs, crops and all the different reining contraptions are not really aids. At the most, they should be considered to be means to reinforce and sometimes to replace the aids. (In a side-saddle the lady has to carry a whip on the right side because both her legs are on the left.) When carrying the reins three and one, the whip should always be carried in the hand that holds the one rein.

I cannot finish this chapter without mentioning the voice, which is an aid just as the others we have discussed. Article 417.4 of the F.E.I. dressage rules says: "The use of the voice in any way whatsoever, or clicking with the tongue once or repeatedly, is a serious fault, involving the deduction of at least two marks from those that would otherwise have been awarded for the movement when this occurred."

As a result of this rule a Swedish competitor in the Grand Prix, during the 1932 Olympic Games in Los Angeles, was put last because of allegedly clicking with the tongue, although he had high

marks. This episode evidently so scared American dressage enthu-
siasts that nobody dared open his mouth. I remember my first
involvement with an American Pony Club in the late 1950s. I was
amazed that nobody ever spoke to his horse.

This was, of course, the result of a misconception. There is an
immense difference between a pony clubber and a Grand Prix rider,
and there is just as big a difference between a young or untrained
horse and a horse with Grand Prix schooling. One should never
forget that there is a difference between the method and the goal.
The goal, of course, is a horse and rider combination that executes
the most difficult movements without anybody hearing or seeing
how the rider influences his horse. Part of the method to achieve
this goal is to use the voice.

Federigo Grisone dedicated a chapter to the use of the voice in *Gli
Ordini di Cavalcare*. And de Pluvinel wrote: "The voice is the spur of
the mind." One of the great advantages of using the voice is that
one can practically do no harm to the horse, which cannot be said
about the other aids. Everybody who lunges knows how fast the
horse learns the meaning of different sounds. Why not take advantage of this, and in the beginning of schooling under saddle get the
horse to walk, trot and canter on voice command? The voice can
have a calming effect on the horse. Therefore, I think that outside
the dressage arena there should be a lot of talking. The words are
not important, but the tone is. My advice is: first speak, then whis-
per, and finally think. This way nobody will hear you.

One can hardly call the clicking of the tongue a voice command,
but it does encourage the horse. In eastern Europe the sound
produced by the vibrating tongue (purring) is the command for a
down transition. I learned this in München-Riem where I heard
Ottokar Pohlman, an East Prussian, making this sound. When I
later tried this with my Polish Trakehner, who had been in America
for several years, I found to my amazement that the horse recog-
nized the sound and responded to it.

Since we are living in an epoch in which mechanics and mecha-
nisation reign supreme, some people seem to forget that the horse is
a living being, which we should respect as such. There are members
of the veterinary profession who disgrace it by forgetting that their
first concern should be the well-being of the horse and not the

ambition or pocketbook of the rider or owner. No veterinarian should act like the pit-crew at a motor-race. If the car has mechanical trouble, the driver pulls into the pits, the mechanics do their job, push the car back on the track and off the driver goes again. A real horseman knows his horse and feels what can be asked of him. Marit Kretschmar in *Pferd und Reiter im Orient* (1980) found that in at least two Turkish epics it was stressed that a commander who broke off a battle because the horses were too tired to go on was praised while two other people were frowned upon. Of these two, one, who had lost his son during a hunt, had kept his horse going during the night in searching for his son and the other had ridden three days and three nights to save his brother. The ethical relationship between man and horse was very strong with the Turks. Times have changed and man is not dependent on horses any more; but this does not mean that we should forget the supreme qualities of this extraordinary living being. The horse is by nature a gentle, non-aggressive animal, only too willing to co-operate, provided however that he is treated with gentleness and firmness. If you treat him as a motorcycle you are in for trouble. Jeanne Boisseau, in *Notes sur l'enseignement de Nuno Oliveira* (1979) quotes a maxim of Oliveira's: "If the horse is happy, everything will be all right; if he is constrained everything will go wrong. And in case that it is necessary to use force, then one enters a domain that does not fit the equestrian art, neither for that matter, in the circle in which civilised people dwell."

I end this chapter urging my readers that we apply the aids to help the horse, not to put him in a mould.

One should avoid resistances, instead of trying to conquer them

AUBERT

Lungeing

One of the practices where misconceptions are rampant is lungeing. There are two reasons for lungeing. One is to benefit the horse; the other is to benefit the rider. It benefits the horse because lungeing is a very important help to school, re-school and to take the edge off a horse that is frisky, possibly because he has not worked very much. As far as the rider is concerned, lungeing will help him find his balance on a moving horse, because the rider does not have to think of the horse and therefore can concentrate exclusively on himself. Lungeing also makes vaulting possible.

For both schooling and vaulting it is essential to have the proper equipment. First, a cavesson made of leather with reinforced noseband is necessary; under no circumstances should a nylon noseband be used. It is irresponsible to hitch the lunge line on to the bit, because we should at all costs avoid hurting the horse in the mouth. Xenophon wrote in *The Art of Horsemanship*: "The groom should also be instructed never to lead the horse on the rein which gives the horse a hard mouth on one side . . .". In an emergency one can use a halter, putting the line through the inside ring of the halter, bringing it over the nose, and then tying the line on to the outside ring. This works as a weak replica of the cavesson.

The lunge line should be about 10 m long, strong and supple and not more than 3 cm wide so that it is easy to handle. There should be no chain at the end of the line. At one end there should be a snap and on the other end a loop, wide enough so that in an emergency the lunger can slip his hand out of the loop. The lunge line should be fastened on to the middle ring of the cavesson. The lunger should take the loop in his outside hand. (When lungeing on the left hand, the lunger's right hand is the outside hand.) The line should not be wound around the hand, as the hand could be caught in the line if the horse runs off. Therefore, one should make a bundle of the line, laying it in the hand, by making figures of eight. The outside hand also carries the whip, while the inside hand guides the horse.

There should be a well-balanced lunge whip available, 2 m long,-

with a lash 30 cm longer. The whip should be used to encourage the horse to move, not by cracking it or by switching it, but by swinging the arm out of the shoulder, similar to casting, as the fisherman does with his fishing rod. After a lot of practise, it should be possible to throw the lash, by an arm movement, to a given spot on the horse's body. If the horse has the inclination to fall into the circle, the whip should be pointed at the shoulder. In case this does not work, one can try to throw the lash towards the horse's head or to make an upward movement with the hand holding the line so that the slack in the line goes to the horse's head.

Before one starts to lunge a young horse, one should realise that it is very important that an atmosphere of confidence exists between the lunger and the young animal. Establishing this atmosphere starts the moment the youngster is handled. There should be no teasing, no beating with whips, no scaring. When a young horse snaps (mainly colts will do this), give him a slap with your hand on his face and say, with much emphasis, "*No*", then pat him. Horses are very sensitive to being patted or stroked, and the voice is also very important. Once the horse has confidence in his master, he will respect and not fear him.

With a totally young horse, the lunger should begin by leading the horse through the arena, to get him acquainted with the surroundings. Then he should lead the horse in a circle, holding the horse close to the head. This can also be done by a helper. Where there is only one person to do the lungeing, he should generally move some distance from the horse, walking on the circle near the hindquarters; he points the whip behind the hindquarters, so that his right arm (holding the whip and the bundle of line) and the left arm (guiding the horse) are similar to the spokes of a wheel. As the horse begins to understand that he is supposed to move on a circle the lunger diminishes his own movements. In this way he becomes the hub of a wheel.

In a circle on the left hand, the lunger's left foot is the inner foot. He lifts it and puts it down on the same spot, similar to a horse doing a turn on the haunches. His outside foot, in this case the right, makes a small circle around the inside foot. This is very important, because the purpose of lungeing is to loosen and decontract the horse so that he will be able to use his back muscles. Therefore, it is necessary to bend the horse laterally, and this is only possible when the horse has to go around an axis, in other words, on a truly round circle. When the lunger keeps walking around, there is no more axis, and consequently no true circle.

The lunger should prevent the horse from leaning on the inside shoulder with his head to the outside. Right from the beginning the horse should learn to bend to the inside. Therefore, the lunger should constantly pull the head in with a gentle movement of the inside arm, bringing the fist towards his chest. This is not a hanging movement, but a give and take movement. The lunger should try to make the horse engage the hindlegs, either with his voice or with the whip. Once the horse has learned to stay on the circle, then the exercises should be done in a lively trot, leading to the working trot.

Is lungeing dangerous? Some veterinarians are strongly against it. One well-known rider claims that it can cause broken legs. My answer is a very categorical "No". Lungeing is not dangerous. In more than 40 years of experience, 20 in the Netherlands and 25 in America, I have never had a lame or injured horse because of lungeing. I have only twice used bandages or ankle boots and only because the owners insisted on it.

There is no better way for the initial schooling of the horse than lungeing. It is important that the horse learns to trot unimpeded by the weight of the rider. The daily routine during a three month period of lungeing should be for 20 minutes at the most. Lungeing should be mostly at the trot alternated with walk to rest and an occasional canter, to strengthen the back muscles and loosen the horse by eliminating contractions.

If the horse is full of energy and wants to canter or gallop at the start of a lesson, let him, so that he gets it out of his system. In this case the lunger should let the line be as long as possible and eventually he can move with the horse. Shortening the line and checking in a rough way can cause damage to the legs, and can break the spirit of the horse. When a horse falls into a trot after a short while, insist on a few more rounds in the canter.

If a horse learns the trick of running away over the outside shoulder, you are in trouble. Mostly he will try to do it in the same spot; in that case move to a side of the arena where he will find a wall. Sometimes it may be necessary to construct a barrier, so that the horse is enclosed.

For horses that tend to be on the forehand or are totally disconnected, I use side-reins with rubber rings: I also use them to let young horses get used to the bit. With horses that carry their heads too high I previously used draw-reins. Lately I have been using the Gogue.

My advice for the use of all these reins is: *be careful*. More horses have been ruined by misuse of these reins than I like to think of. If you decide to use them, begin by having them as long as possible and gradually shorten them. Do not try to collect a horse by tightening the side-reins, and do not try to force the head down by shortening the draw-reins or the Gogue. If you do, you are really asking for trouble. There is nothing a horse hates more than being constrained; he will either fight it or surrender and come into a faulty frame.

As a guide to the diameter of the lunge circle, it should be such that with the correct equipment the trainer is able to just touch the horse with the end of the lash when handling the whip in the proper manner.

In this chapter I have tried to describe how to go about lungeing, and the misconceptions and pitfalls one may encounter. A treatise about lungeing riders and about vaulting is outside the scope of this book.

Nature did not make a horse to all the time go on circles and on two tracks; for a young horse it is better to be kept for a long time on a straight line

ROUSSELET, SPEAKING TO L'HOTTE

The Purpose and the Importance of the Circle

The reason why the circle is one of the first schooling movements is that it introduces the horse to lateral flexions, therefore it is very important that the rider really tries to bend, or flex, the horse around the inside leg. The horse cannot follow the track of the circle if he is not flexed. It is very important that the circle is ridden in the middle of the arena with B and E as the tangents. Most horses will try to stick on the railing when they reach B or E, therefore, the teacher has to make sure that the horse stays flexed and just touches B and E. When the horse has learned to stay flexed throughout the circle, the rider can try to ride the circle at A or C. The difficulty is that, coming so close to the corners, the horse goes into the corners and loses the curve. When this happens the purpose of riding the circle is lost, because the horse straightens. In a dressage test this means a low mark.

After the horse has, for a certain period of time, been lunged in the appropriate way, it will not be very difficult to ride a twenty metre diameter circle. As the required diameter is reduced, the difficulties will increase because the horse has to curve more. Therefore if the circle is larger than required in the test, the score will be lower, because the rider is avoiding the difficulty of the prescribed movement.

In order to teach the horse to go on the circle, it is helpful if he has learned to yield to pressure of the outside rein against the neck, so that he brings his shoulders on the track of the circle. A vibrating inside rein, so that the rider sees the shimmer of the inside eye will cause flexing of the poll, allowing the horse to look in the direction in which he will be going. Pushing the inside knee down will cause more pressure of the inside seat–bone, an inside calf closed just behind the girth will help in creating impulsion. It is a great help if the rider slightly rotates the spinal column, thereby pointing the shoulders and the hips in the direction he wants the horse to go. Initially the outside leg has a passive role, namely preventing the haunches from swinging out, but as the diameter is reduced, for 15 metre, 10 metre and 8 metre circles, and finally the 6 metre volte, the outside leg becomes more active as the flexion has to increase.

It is essential that the outside rein allows the horse to follow the arc of the circle, if that rein is too tight, the horse cannot curve. It is also essential that the rider does not pull with the inside rein as that would cause the horse to go on the outside shoulder.

When riding circles, the rider should never forget that its purpose is to flex the horse laterally in order to loosen him.

The highest mark should be given when the influence of the rider is invisible. Because of the fact that many riders have a deficient seat, they try to compensate this by increasing the use of the hands and the legs

KURT ALBRECHT

The Walk

La Guérinière makes a distinction between two kinds of walk: the "pas de campagne" and the "pas d'école". In a later chapter I shall go deeper into the details of the "pas d'école", the school walk. It is a diagonal movement that, in the seventeenth and eighteenth centuries, was strictly used in an equitational context. General Decarpentry condemned this movement severely in his book *Equitation Académique* (1947).

I would like to describe the "pas de campagne" as a natural, normal walk, a gait in which there are always three feet on the ground and in which there are no floating moments. (De Kunffy calls it an earthbound gait.) During this walk the horse moves freely, unconstrainedly, he is not loitering. It is used while hacking, and when used by the cavalry, had a tempo of 100 metres per minute. During this walk, the rider has a light elastic contact. (See Chapter 3.)

The discussions in the German Cavalry Manual of 1912 of the working trot and the working canter are very explicit about the walk: "As far as the walk is concerned, greatest attention should be given to the creation and maintenance of a correct and pure walk; therefore premature and strong resistance with the reins should be avoided. An incorrect, uneven and dragging walk will improve most of the time after the horse has learned to trot properly."

In the rules of the F.E.I. one can read in Article 403, 3: ". . . a horse should not be asked to walk 'on the bit' at the early stages of his training. A too precipitous collection will not only spoil the collected walk, but the medium and the extended as well."

I am amazed that after these wise words the F.E.I. in rule 403, 4.1 in describing the collected walk, says, among other things, ". . . that the horse, 'remaining on the bit' moves resolutely forward, with the neck raised and arched. The head approaches the vertical position. The hindlegs are engaged with good hock action." The amazing thing is that for the collected trot and the collected canter similar expressions are being used.

What the authors of the rules have overlooked is that the walk is not only a four-beat movement, but that it is also different from both the trot and the canter, in that, while walking, the head moves forward and backward in the rhythm of the four-beat movement.

I wonder if it makes sense at all to ask for a collected walk. The F.E.I. has for all three gaits the same wording when the requirements for collection are described. Namely: "a raised and arched neck and good hock action." I do not believe that during the walk the horse is able to raise and arch the neck and have good hock action.

When the rider during the walk, increases or decreases, *always in an elastic way*, the tension in the reins, the horse will shorten or lengthen the stride. The shortening of the stride is necessary to prepare the horse to execute a correct turn on the haunches.

When the rider increases the resistance of the guiding aids together with increasing the driving aids, the result will be either a square halt or a diagonal movement such as the trot, the school walk, the piaffe or the passage, all depending on the interplay between the driving aids and the guiding aids, orchestrated by the equestrian tact of the rider.

The trot is a diagonal movement, the alternating forward–upward pushing of the hindlegs causes a moment that all four legs are off the ground. It is a *floating* moment during the trot and the school walk and a moment of *suspension* during piaffe and passage.

Because the hindlegs can come further under the body carrying more of the load, the horse can elevate the forehand and raise the neck, thereby striking an impressive pose. That is what we want to see in collection. It is kinesiologically impossible for an earthbound gait.

Basically the walk is a gait of relaxation. The real work in the walk comes when extension is asked for. This exercise however, should only be asked for during the schooling for higher levels. In the first year the walk should be strictly a movement of decontraction, lively and free. During the periods after strenuous trot or canter exercises the walk should be a period of rest. This does not mean that the horse should be allowed to loiter. He should stay on a straight line and the rider should forego the temptation of trying to put the horse's head in position or of trying to elevate the forehand.

If the rider succumbs to the temptation to monkey with his hands, there is a great chance that the horse will not accept the bit, will start tossing the head, will lose the push from his hindquarters and possibly start pacing.

The trot is the gait at which to gymnasticise the horse because during this movement he has two feet diagonally on the ground and two feet diagonally in the air, alternated by a floating moment. Once the back muscles have been strengthened the rider can begin to ask for collection in the trot.

Only after the horse has learned to collect during the trot can one begin to ask for extensions. The extended walk is a very difficult movement. It is not very often that one sees a correct extension, even in Grand Prix. Most of the time the riders allow their horses a "free walk on the long rein". The movement lacks the impetus from the push of the hindlegs that is necessary for an extended walk. My belief is that the reason for this poor showing lies in the fact that most riders lack the knowledge of what aids have to be used to achieve this movement. It has become an axiom that if one wants a horse to get moving or to lengthen, the rider has to use his legs, but this is not always the case. One can use too much leg and then some horses will not respond at all. René Gogue in *Problèmes Equestres* (1978) makes clear that the rotating of the pelvis in the rhythm of the movement of the walk, so that the seat-bone on the side of the forward moving hindleg helps the movement by pushing forward, is the logical way to help the horse develop the extended walk. According to Gogue, this rotating of the pelvis is also the best way to develop the piaffe. This rotating has nothing in common with the "massaging of the horse's back" advised by some other contemporary authors. My personal experience proves that Gogue's suggestion is effective.

The best bit is the one in wise hands

GENERAL L'HOTTE

The Free Walk

A serious observer who watches the free walk in the lower level dressage tests will come to the conclusion that it is not easy to find any consistency in the manner in which it is performed by the various entries. Some horses will loiter while doing the movement, looking left and right, on a totally loose rein; others will go more or less straight on a loose rein, but at the moment the rider starts to adjust the reins in preparation for the next movement, the horse starts to jog. Then there are riders who have their horses go pretty nicely, with moderate action from behind, but still no rein contact, because they think the horse has to be free. It can be too free, as I have twice experienced while judging, when nicely moving horses stopped on the diagonal to scratch their heads on a foreleg.

I think that the confusion is caused by the misinterpretation of the word "free" in the context of a dressage test. Free in this context does not mean a free horse. It does mean a free movement: a movement that is decontracted, because there are no tensions and there is no constraint.

Another reason for the confusion is the wording in the A.H.S.A. rule book (1982–83) Article 3–4e states: "The free walk is a pace of relaxation in which the horse is allowed complete freedom to lower and stretch out his head and neck. The hindfeet touch the ground clearly in front of the footprints of the forefeet . . ." This rule is in accordance with the F.E.I. rule, Article 403,4–4 with the exception that the F.E.I. does not ask that: "The hindfeet touch the ground clearly in front of the footprints of the forefeet." The only time that the F.E.I. asks for this is in the extended walk. This makes sense, because there are a lot of horses whose conformation makes it very difficult to fulfil this requirement of tracking up. For those horses a lot of schooling is required to get them to track up, and there is no chance that they will be able to do it during relaxation. I do not think that it is fair to ask, during a period of relaxation, that the horse perform a movement that is practically impossible to execute, because of his conformation.

Since dressage competition first began, one of the difficulties has been to achieve unity in terminology. People from different countries with different doctrines were part of the committees that organised dressage. The old rule books never had very much to say about the walk. For a long time there was the ordinary walk, (French "pas ordinaire") and the strong or extended walk (French "pas allongé") and, of course, the collected walk (French "pas rassemblé"). In the *German Cavalry Manual* (1912) a collected walk is mentioned, and a free walk in which 125 strides per minute had to be made. This proves that this walk was purely for military marches; it was called free because the horse had to be unconstrained during this movement. Seunig equates this free walk with the medium or ordinary walk.

In 1936, the Grand Prix test to be ridden during the Olympic Games contained a movement called "Freier Schritt", or free walk. When one reads the test it becomes clear that this free walk could not be a gait of relaxation. The test reads in part: "At C, on the right hand, collected trot to B, at B free walk on the long rein, at F turn right, at K turn to the left in the collected walk with adjusted reins."

In contemporary terminology it would have said: "At B medium walk on a long rein, at K collected walk."

As I hope to show in the next chapter, it was in 1975 that a rational terminology was agreed upon.

There is a saying that the horse should enjoy himself in his work, otherwise neither the rider nor the horse would be able to give an elegant performance

PLUVINEL

8 The Working Trot

Since the trot is the most important gait as far as the gymnasticising of horses is concerned, rule book terminology has changed very much over the years in describing it.

All the misconceptions and fallacies surrounding the working trot are proof that it is one thing to translate a foreign term literally and quite another thing to understand its meaning.

The A.H.S.A. rule book (1982–3) describes the working trot as "a regular and unconstrained trot, in which a horse, not yet trained and ready for collected movements, shows himself properly balanced ...". My question is: how can a horse that is not yet trained show himself in proper balance? Since the working trot is a schooling movement, it cannot really be covered by a definition. It has to be made clear to the riders what the purpose of this schooling movement is; namely, to activate the hindquarters and to get the horse steadily on the bit. This is a process in which a horse learns to trot in a steady, balanced way. Horses in the wild walk long distances when they move from one grazing place to another. They will trot a little when they play, and they may even do a few steps of passage when they want to impress. When there is danger, they will gallop. Therefore, what we really have to do is to teach the horse to trot in a consistent way, not just to play. Since the trot is the most efficient movement for the gymnasticising of the horse (only two legs at the same time being on the ground), we have to begin to teach him this gait and work on it until we have a horse that, to quote Bourgelat, "trots with impulse, being decontracted and in balance".

When we have achieved this, then the time has arrived for the real schooling work: suppling exercises, lateral and longitudinal flexions, and all the more difficult movements.

In the more than 50 years that the F.E.I. has given guidance to dressage, a lot of thought has been put into the writing of the rules and tests. During that process different doctrines collided with each other. The result was, most of the time, compromise. However,

69

when one peruses the successive rule books, an evolution is also noticeable.

The following short survey may help clarify many of the misunderstandings and the general confusion existing around the different kinds of trot. The data available are the texts of the F.E.I. Grand Prix de Dressage of 1928 (German); 1936 (German and French); 1948 (German and French); 1967 (German, French and English) and the rule books of the F.E.I. 1938 (German and French); 1950 (French and English); 1958 (French and English); 1963 (French and English); 1971 (French and English); 1975 (French and English); 1983 (French and English).

1928	abgekürzter Trab		starker Trab
	short trot		extended trot
1936	abgekürzter Trab	Mitteltrab	starker Trab
	short trot	ordinary trot	extended trot
1948	versammelter Trab	Arbeitstrab	Mitteltrab
	trot rassemblé	trot ordinaire	trot allongé
	collected trot	ordinary trot	extended trot
1950	trot rassemblé	trot ordinaire	trot allongé
	collected trot	ordinary trot	extended trot
1958	same as 1950		
1963	versammelter Trab	Mitteltrab	starker Trab
	trot rassemblé	trot moyen	trot allongé
	collected trot	ordinary trot	extended trot
1967	same as 1963		
1971	same as 1963 and 1967		

1975	versammelter Trab	Arbeitstrab	Mitteltrab	starker Trab
	trot rassemblé	trot de travail	trot moyen	trot allongé
	collected trot	working trot	medium trot	extended trot
1982	same as 1975			

The F.E.I. rule books 1948 and 1950 give the same definition of the ordinary trot; we read under # 171 ed. 1950: "Ordinary trot (natural, as normally used in road work). This is a pace between the extended and the collected trot. The horse goes forward freely and straight, goes well off the hocks, softly into his bridle, with a balanced and free action. The steps should be as even as possible and the hindfeet should follow exactly in the tracks of the forefeet."

A very important note is added: "The ordinary trot must not be confused with the Mitteltrab (German), a trot with a more elevated and energetic action, with increased flexion of all joints, it is a brilliant trot, which the horse is taught."

The rule book of 1958 gives the same definition. However, it adds the following: "The degree of energy and impulsion displayed at the ordinary trot denotes clearly the degree of suppleness and balance of the horse." The 1950 note, of course, is omitted. Consequently, the French text of 1963 has replaced "trot ordinaire" with "trot moyen", and the French text of the Grand Prix now also uses "pas moyen" and "galop moyen". For their national tests the French now also use "trot moyen".

As the above survey makes clear, 1975 brought important changes: the working trot is introduced and the English version of the rule book abandons the term ordinary trot and replaces it with medium trot. So, twelve years after the concept of "trot ordinaire" was dropped from the French version of the rule book and replaced by "trot moyen", the English version accepted the new concept and used the term "medium trot".

The very lucid description Hermann Friedländer gives of the working trot, in *Chronicle of the Horse* (1970), makes it clear that the working trot is something different than the ordinary trot, described in 1950 as "natural, as normally used in road work". It indeed is called a working trot, because the horse has to work in order to be able to execute a rhythmic, balanced trot, using all his muscles, so that he finally will be able not only to perform the trot as normally used in road work, but also that he can be schooled in the whole scale of the different trots. Working trot is in the first place a schooling gait. Although the Germans have an equivalent for ordinary trot, "Gebrauchstrab", they do not ask for it in dressage tests. Seunig sees the "Gebrauchstrab", a trot for practical

71

use, as the end result of working trot, medium trot and a shortened trot. He emphasises that collected, medium and extended trot are pure dressage gaits. Dressage riding has a very broad foundation in Germany and, because of the still strong influence of the former military riding, there is one school of thought with which every German who starts riding is confronted. All are as familiar with these terms as with the alphabet, while foreigners are not.

In deciding what terms to use it, of course, makes a lot of sense to follow the F.E.I. terminology; it is up to the instructors and the riders to become familiar with the meaning of all these concepts by seriously studying them.

It is too, up to the judges to stress in their commentary the importance of the engagement of the hindquarters. Without this engagement there will be no balanced rhythmic trot; there will be no pure gait.

When, due to his conformation, one can only expect a limited extension from a horse, one should, if the movement is correct and rhythmic, evaluate this performance as high as the impressive lengthening of a horse that was born with this talent

KURT ALBRECHT

Lengthening of the Stride and Extending the Trot

Since the basic principles and common misconceptions about lengthening of the stride and extending the trot are the same, the problems can be dealt with in one chapter.

The old masters did not know an extended trot. Their concern was only to get the haunches under the horse, because originally in man-to-man battle the forehand had to come off the ground. This later developed into the school jumps, although it did not prevent these horses from going very well cross-country, after a little schooling. This is illustrated in a story told by Gaspar de Saunier (1756). Louis XIV, preparing to go on a campaign during one of his many wars, ordered that 40 horses be chosen from the stables in Versailles. They were Turkish, Berber and Spanish horses which had been exclusively schooled to do the school jumps. For the coming campaign they had to be prepared to go over rough country and to jump ditches. The beginning was very difficult; they stumbled, sometimes fell on their knees, and had difficulties keeping themselves up. They refused to jump, and even refused to go near ditches. The riders dismounted and tied a rope to the cavesson. This rope was held by a man on the other side of the ditch (in the way Xenophon had already described). When they finally had learned to jump the ditches while mounted, they proved themselves better than the best hunters, not only because of their speed, but also because of their stability on their legs in all sorts of country and also jumping ditches and hedges.

As far as I know, La Guérinière was the first to mention something that implies lengthening. He writes about a lively trot in which the horse lengthens himself ("hardi et étendu") in order to loosen the shoulders and the hindquarters. He advises using this trot when there is trouble teaching the shoulder-in.

75

After the French Revolution, there developed in Europe an interest in the English Thoroughbred and the way the English rode in the field. As a result, we find in the literature the beginning of the description of the strong trot (French "grand trot", German "starker Trab"). For example Hünersdorf (1800) writes about the lengthening of the stride ("ausgedehnter Trab"). He claims that the advantage of this movement is that the horse learns how to lengthen himself, is strengthened by these exercises, and is taught to go forward with head and neck correctly placed.

The Comte d'Aure (1852) wrote that speed is not obtained by allowing the horse to go forward in an impetuous way. The fact that d'Aure asks a group of riders to execute the lengthened trot ("trot allongé") on a circle proves that the length of this trot was far less than the length of the modern extended trot. Nowadays, the extended trot is not being asked on the circle, because it is impossible. Rather, it is the medium trot that now is asked on the circle.

Von Oeynhausen (1852) stresses that the trot be pure, which means that the diagonal feet are lifted and put down at the same moment. He wants the movement lively and diligent.

Faverot de Kerbrech (1891), interpreter of Baucher, writes that the strong trot ("grand trot") should be progressively developed out of the ordinary trot ("petit trot"). The movement should be free and resolute; the head should be close to the perpendicular, and the horse should go energetically and straight forward.

When reading these quotations, one has to remember that the authors lived during an era when the basics of equitation were still the engaging of the hindquarters and gymnasticising of the back. It is my opinion that the F.E.I. was stimulated by Caprilli to ask for extending movements in the dressage tests in order to get the riders out of the habit of pulling their horses together. I think that a misconceived interpretation of Caprilli is at the root of bad extensions. Caprilli wanted the horse unconstrained in going cross-country, so that the neck and back could be used. Unconstrained does not mean that the horse should go without any contact with the rider's hand, resulting in a disconnected horse. It does mean that the rider has an elastic contact with always straight reins "never" loops and with the tension varying from featherlight to firm. The horse does not object to firm contact as long as it is elastic; the horse resents and often fights a dead hand, one that is set or is pulling. With this elastic contact, the rider is able to keep the horse in balance.

When either a lengthening of the stride or an extension is asked for in dressage competitions, one sees only too frequently that the rider lets go, losing all contact. The result is that the horse falls apart and loses his balance, because the hindlegs do not push any more and they spread far apart. To some it may give the impression of a lengthened frame, but it is a functionally incorrect lengthening, because the hindlegs do not push, the back is not engaged; as a result the horse loses his balance resulting in rushing or coming on the forehand. A sure way to find out if the horse lengthens in a functionally correct way is to ask him to trot over cavalletti or to jump a low obstacle out of the trot. Most mistakes of allowing the horse to "fall into two pieces" can be corrected once the rider understands what lengthening of the stride and extension really mean. A far more serious mistake is to allow the horse to throw his front legs in the air and let them not only touch the ground later than the diagonal hindleg, but also bring the front feet back. In other words, the front foot is not touching the ground on the spot at which the foot, in its highest elevation, pointed. This is a difficult mistake to correct, because it is a movement that quite a few horses offer. To the layman it looks elegant, and the public thinks it is spectacular. For that reason, the judges may tend to overlook it. This movement is the result of a stiff back in the horse, and that is where the correction should begin.

According to the F.E.I. rule book (Article 404, 4.4) in the extended trot: "The horse covers as much ground as possible. Maintaining the same cadence (rhythm), he lengthens his steps to the utmost as a result of great impulsion from the hindquarters. The rider allows the horse, remaining on the bit, without leaning on it, to lengthen his frame and to gain ground. The forefeet should touch the ground on the spot towards which they are pointing." It has to be emphasised that it is the lengthening of the steps that should be the main concern. That is what the judges have to look at. The lengthening of the frame is secondary, because it is the result of the lengthening of the steps.

It is a misconception that in the extended trot the horse should put his nose forward. The aforementioned rule does not speak of either the nose or the head. The misconception is caused by the fact that for the extended canter the rule book mentions: ". . . the tip of the nose pointing more or less forward."

In this connection it is interesting that Faverot de Kerbrech wrote that the head should be close to perpendicular. In the *German Cavalry Manual* (1912) I find a picture of a horse in the extended trot with his head nearly perpendicular. The misconception that the nose be allowed to come forward may well be the reason that so many horses lose their balance or "fall in two pieces", which is worse. According to Egon von Neindorff, with whom I had a discussion about this subject several years ago, the horse loses the maximum forward drive of the hindlegs if the rider allows the nose to come forward. And this maximum forward drive is what the rules ask for: ". . . he lengthens his steps to the utmost as a result of great impulsion from the hindquarters."

A special problem is encountered with some of the European Warmblood horses. When asked to perform an extended trot they show something that is very spectacular: they float over the ground and barely seem to touch it because they show very distinct suspension. Sometimes it looks like an extended passage. It is a way of going the horse offers, not the result of schooling. At every stallion show in Europe, when they are shown in hand, one can see this way of movement. It is, of course, difficult to penalise something so spectacular, but I think we should, because this way of going is functionally incorrect.

It seems to me that rule 404 of the F.E.I. causes confusion by saying: "The trot is a pace of two time on alternate diagonals (. . .) separated by a moment of suspension." This can be, and is frequently interpreted, as if cadence, a prolonged suspension was being asked for. For this reason it might be better not to talk about suspension but a floating movement. I do not think that the trot is pure when the movement is not continuous. To suspend means, in a broad sense, to stop temporarily, to cause to cease or to bring to a stop.

This momentary stopping is what happens in the piaffe and in the passage, this is also the trot the Hackney is famous for. I do not

78

think that a trot with a moment of holding back is the trot for a riding horse.

It should be stressed that, when asking for the extended trot, the rider should never lean backwards. It is not only awful to watch from an aesthetic viewpoint, it is also functionally incorrect. It is also a misconception to think that the rider has to put his weight backwards in order to engage the hindquarters. The rider's centre of gravity behind the plumbline prevents the horse from swinging his hindlegs well forward. At all times the rider has to be with the movement of the horse and not behind it. The trouble is, of course, that most of the great champions do lean back, and what champions do is imitated by those less fortunate.

In a dressage competition the focus is on the performance of the rider–horse combination, the unity of this combination and the willingness and the ability of the horse to respond to the rider's indications; in breed classes, the extravagance of the movements may be a point of consideration.

To recapitulate: in either the lengthening of the stride or in the extended trot, the rider should drive to create impulsion in the movement of the horse, and he should maintain the contact with the horse's mouth in order to prevent the horse from losing his balance. In the extended trot he should also be sure to prevent the nose from coming forward in order to get the maximum push from the hindquarters.

Finally I would like to quote part of F.E.I. rule book, Chapter II, Article 420, 4: "The test includes all the school paces and all the fundamental airs of the Classical High School, of which the fancy (author translation) paces, based on extreme extension of the forelegs are no part . . ."

Illustration Plates

PLATE I
The author competing in Rome, 1937

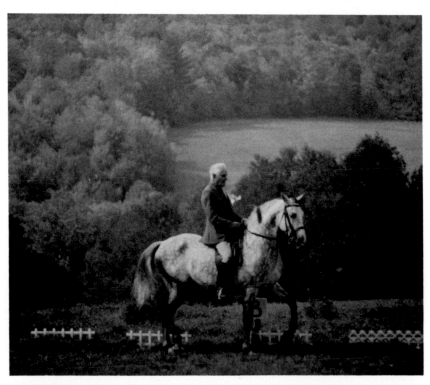

PLATE 2
A more leisurely pace at home in Cavendish, New England, 1979

PLATE 3
Sigmund von Josipovich

PLATE 4
Egon von Neindorff on Jaguar

PLATE 5
Geza von Haszlinszky, of the Spanish Riding School, demonstrates piaffer

PLATE 6
. . . and passage

5

PLATE 7
A pupil of von Neindorff; impeccable position

PLATE 8
Rider leaning backwards. A sight one sees only too often, even at the highest level of competition

6

PLATE 9
Stretching elbows

PLATE 10
Hands "playing the piano" resulting in the elbows being too far from the body and preventing a supple elbow movement

PLATE 11
Hands carrying the reins "three-and-one"

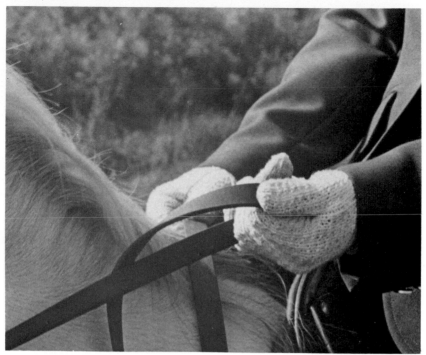

PLATE 12
A gentle upward rotation of the inside hand to see the inside eye. Inside rein close to the neck; outside rein against the neck, while vibrating the inside rein in order to see the shimmer of the inside eye

PLATE 13
Madame de Padirac

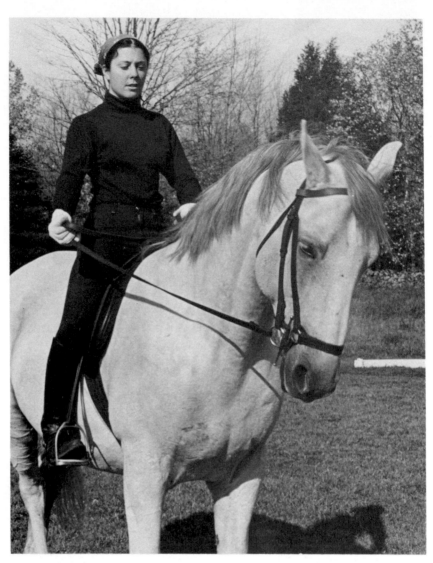

PLATE 14
Applying opening rein

PLATE 15
Hollow back

PLATE 18
A drawing reproduced from a frame of a film of Egon von Neindorff's stallion Jaguar. This horse covers as much ground as possible, he lengthens his steps to the utmost as a result of great impulsion from the hindquarters. According to von Neindorff he can bring his hindlegs far under, because his head is being kept perpendicular

OPPOSITE PAGE

PLATE 16 (top)
A horse that is on the forehand while the hindquarters are too high. The reason for this is very likely that the horse cannot bring the hindquarters under because of anatomical shortcomings. He cannot flex his hocks adequately, therefore the croup goes up and the shoulders down

PLATE 17 (below)
A drawing done from a picture of a horse being ridden by Waldemar Seunig. This is an example of the idea that the nose should come slightly forward. Because the nose is forward, one gets the impression of the horse becoming long in the frame, with the risk of falling apart

PLATE 19

The rider is preventing the horse from looking to the outside. The elbow is stretched so that the forward movement is not impeded

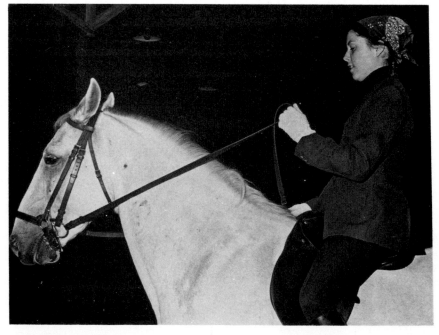

PLATE 20

The elbow is broken and the forward movement is impeded

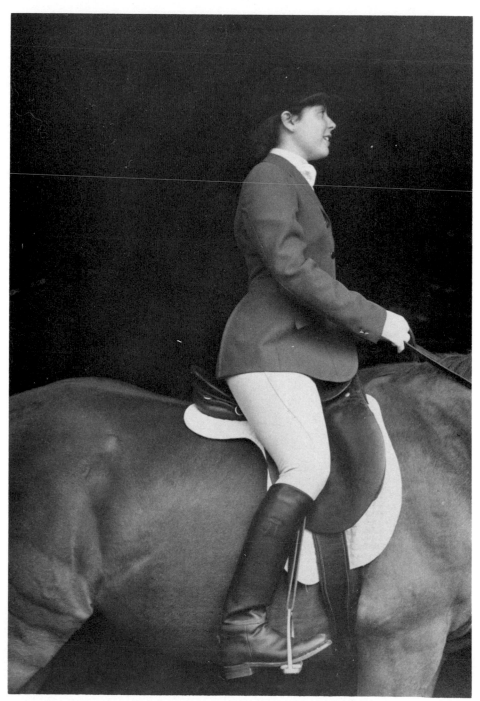

PLATE 21
Here the rider has the knee too deep and sits on top of the saddle

PLATE 22
Bracing the backbone

Nothing good can be achieved without tempo and rhythm

CESARE FIASCHI

Tempo, Rhythm, Cadence

Since I believe that there is a lot of confusion about the exact meaning of "tempo", "rhythm" and "cadence" I want in this chapter to try to define them.

All three terms are used in music, dance and verse. However, one does not find always clear–cut definitions for them in dictionaries. Very often, rhythm and cadence are considered to be virtually the same, and also are quite often regarded as interchangeable. The following definitions are, therefore, applicable to equitation only.

Tempo is the speed over a certain distance. For example: in the military, the tempo for the walk was 100 m per minute; for the trot 200 m per minute; for the canter 350 m per minute. The rules for combined training specify the tempo for the steeplechase to be 690 m per minute. When the horse is asked to extend, he is supposed to cover more ground; that is what is called the increasing of the tempo. The horse should not increase the frequency of the movement, or, as the F.E.I. rule book says (Article 404.4) should be "maintaining the same rhythm". (Changed in 1983 to cadence.)

Rhythm is a fluent sequence of movements in a certain beat. When a horse misses a beat or when the length of the strides becomes uneven, the horse loses rhythm.

Instead of giving cadence almost the same meaning as rhythm, I suggest using this term in reference to movements of prolonged suspension, such as piaffe and passage. The F.E.I. rule book says in Articles 413 and 414 that these movements should be "very cadenced" or "highly cadenced" and with "prolonged suspension". Lately, one sees more and more that in the extended trot the front legs are thrown out with some suspension. This cadence in the extended trot may be spectacular, but it is against the rules and it is functionally incorrect. The purpose of the lengthening of the stride, and eventually of achieving an extended trot, is to show that the horse is able to lengthen and shorten his frame. This, of course, is what makes the horse more versatile. I would like to see a horse in a "cadenced extended trot" go at an obstacle.

Riders should form a clear idea about these expressions, because, in the schooling of a horse and eventually in riding a test, they should be able to maintain an even tempo, rhythm and, in passage and piaffe, cadence. Often in lower tests, one sees that horses sometimes go faster, sometimes slower. This is seen especially after a turn; for example, from B across the arena to E. The horses go faster because they fall apart.

In the trot, especially, the rhythm should be lively and well accentuated. The sequence of the movements should be continuous. When there are moments of prolonged suspension (for example the trot of the Hackney), then the trot is cadenced.

When the horse does not engage the hindquarters, has a stiff back, or when the movement is dull, then there is no lively and accentuated rhythm. The rhythm is also lost when the beat is uneven. This can, of course, be caused by uneven footing; it generally is, however, the result of the fact that the horse does not carry himself.

Cadence, as I interpret it, is only asked for in the piaffe and in the passage. Because of the prolonged suspension, the sequence of the rhythmic movements is not continuous. That makes the difference with the pure trot. What pure trot and passage and piaffe have in common is that they all three should be rhythmic. A piaffe in which the movements are continuous is not correct, because there is no prolonged suspension. One sees this faulty piaffe only too often, especially when the rider in desperation makes more movements than the horse.

To conclude: even tempo, rhythm and cadence can only be achieved by a horse that engages the hindquarters, carries himself and is permeable.

A good hand is the one that can resist and yield when necessary and receive with precision the action created by the legs

SALOMON DE LA BROUE

1 Leg-yielding

There is a lot of confusion regarding the exercises shoulder-in and leg-yielding. This confusion has been stimulated by a statement, made by an influential teacher, that when the test asks for a shoulder-in and the horse executes a correct leg-yielding, he would consider the movement to be sufficient.

I hope to make it clear that shoulder-in and leg-yielding are two totally different exercises. Leg-yielding supples or loosens the hindquarters, but brings the horse on the forehand. Shoulder-in supples or loosens the shoulders and engages the inner hindleg. It was because of the limited effect that leg-yielding had on the overall suppling of the horse, that la Guérinière looked for a better way and as a result of his reflections invented shoulder-in.

According to the old Masters, leg-yielding has a lot of drawbacks. For example Waldemar Seunig in *Am Pulsschlag der Reitkunst* (1961) had this to say about leg-yielding: "Leg-yielding's purpose is preparation for two track work. The advantage in preparing two track work, just as well attainable by other less dangerous exercises, is generally outweighed by these disadvantages:

A) Because the horse is being ridden on a slightly wider track without bending, full development of vigorous use of the hindlegs is hampered and a loss of pure gait is very possible even with sensitive riders.

B) The hindlegs do not support enough because they are not yet able to tread under and therefore move outside of, the track of the front legs instead of forward in the direction of the centre of gravity. The horse, stumbling sideways instead of moving forward and sideways, loses poise and rhythm and falls on the shoulder.

C) The fact that the forehand does not precede the haunches during the sideways movement gives rise to the danger that, while stepping over, the inside front leg will hit the outside front leg, causing spavins."

Under the influence of Seunig's book, leg-yielding was dropped from the dressage tests in 1964, and soon afterward the turn on the forehand out of the standstill was also dropped.

Long before Seunig, Louis Seeger wrote in his book, *System der Reitkunst* (1844), that the shoulder-in is the best exercise to teach a horse to be obedient to the leg, to yield to the leg. What nowadays is called leg-yielding Seeger refers to as "head-in, haunches-out". He is against this movement because it brings the horse on the forehand, and since the legs have to cross each other they are in each other's way, thus hindering the movement. Seeger, like Seunig, warns about the risks of lameness resulting from this movement. Such risks include shoulder lameness, which can be caused when the shoulder is pulled forcibly inwards and sometimes forward in direct antagonism to the pectoral muscles; bowed tendons caused by strain on the ligaments and tendon sheaths of the front legs; stepping on the coronet band caused by the crossing action of the front legs, and thickness of the knees caused by straining of the bursa of the tendon surrounding the knee-joint.

Gustav Steinbrecht in *Das Gymnasium des Pferdes* (1884) wrote: "Two track movement without bending and collection are always wrong exercises." He also warns about the lameness Seeger was concerned about and he includes splints, which can also be caused by strain on the surrounding ligaments or trauma to the splint-bone area. Notwithstanding these warnings of the old Masters, leg-yielding has been reintroduced as a schooling movement, and institutionalised as a test movement.

Oberbereiter von Niedermayer (1837–1887), quoted by Podhajsky, stated that head-in, hindquarters-out, could only have been invented by human want of judgement. Applied unreasonably and without moderation, this exercise is damaging for every horse (Niedermayer). Podhajsky in *Die Klassische Reitkunst* (1965) states emphatically that the turn on the forehand and leg-yielding do not belong in classical exercises; they can never be more than an expedient. For this reason, they should never be asked for in a dressage test, not even for beginners.

Nobody contests that the horse should be obedient to the leg and eventually yield to the leg. But this loosening exercise should never be done on the straightaway. The reason that leg-yielding on the circle is beneficial is because the horse does not lose impulsion, the centrifugal force taking care of this. What on the straight line becomes a stumbling movement becomes on the circle a rhythmical movement in which the inner hindleg can swing well over the outer hindleg, while on the straight the swing can only be moderate. Therefore it is only on the circle that leg-yielding becomes a real suppling exercise for the hindquarters. To quote Podhajsky about leg-yielding: "On the circle and only for basic schooling."

On the straight line and on the diagonal the inside leg is limited in how far it can step over. I have the impression that this is the reason why those who practise leg-yielding excessively on the diagonal generally make very poor half-passes.

It is incomprehensible to me that anybody could have thought up such a movement as leg-yielding on the diagonal which has a disastrous effect on the half-pass, this is the leaning on the shoulder, in the direction of travel. Later, in the half-pass, this is the gravest mistake because the horse then has to be bent and look in the direction he is going.

To execute leg-yielding on the circle, one should tighten the outside rein, the hand a little up and press the rein against the neck in order to push the shoulders in on the circle. In this way the shoulders of the horse are stabilised so that they can function as a kind of mobile pivot around which the haunches can turn. If the rider tries to get the horse on the circle by using the inside rein, he will stop the forward movement if he applies the direct rein of opposition (pulls), he will destabilise the shoulders if he applies the opening rein, pulling the head in. The taut outside rein will cause a slight bend. The inside leg presses well behind the girth. The rider has to push the outside knee deep so that there is more weight on the outside seat-bone. In the beginning, after two sideways movements of the horse's hindquarters, one should go straight with little tension in the reins, making the horse go well forward. After a few strides straight forward, one asks for yielding to the other leg. In case the horse has difficulties understanding what he is supposed to do, a helper should use his fist in the place where the rider's leg is supposed to act. This exercise should be limited to the beginning of the schooling period, until the horse is able to make half-circles stepping well over. The circles are on two tracks.

By tightening the outside rein and pressing this rein well against the neck, a half turn on the forehand can be developed. If one insists on making turns on the forehand, this is a better way than first letting the horse come to a halt, allowing it to lose impulsion, and then trying to make this turn with a lot of pounding with the heels. While the latter may be a pragmatic procedure, it is certainly not an equitational one.

The rider who asks for leg-yielding should be well aware of the fact that the sole purpose of this exercise is the suppling of the hindquarters. He should try to avoid combining this exercise with any other exercise, because it will totally confuse the horse.

A last word of caution: the horse can only engage the hindlegs if they move on a straight line. When the inner hindleg steps over the outer hindleg, the hindquarters swing out. When the inner hindleg steps in front of the outer hindleg, the hindquarters can still stay on a straight line. When the hindquarters swing out, they cannot push any more and the movement becomes defective. I am convinced that a lot of the poor movements one sees all too often are the result of an overevaluating of the need to practise leg-yielding.

It is not the speed, neither the number of strides, that should be evaluated during the pirouette, but it is the rhythm of the jumps and the maintenance of the balance during the turns

HANS VON HEYDEBRECK

2 The Turn on the Haunches and the Pirouette

Since the turn on the haunches leads to the pirouette, the execution of both these movements reveals the same basic shortcomings most of the time. For this reason, it is possible to discuss both these movements in the same chapter. The difference between the two movements, according to the rule book, is that in the pirouette the inner hindfoot should come down in the same spot, or slightly in front; in the turn on the haunches, the inner hindfoot is not required to come down in the same spot but may move slightly forward.

The very important requisite of both movements is that the inner hindleg should make distinct steps, and the inner hindfoot should not stick to the ground (pivoting). Very often one sees this pivoting on the inner hindfoot and, maybe more often, pivoting on the outside hindfoot, when the horse shifts his weight to the outside.

I am convinced that faulty execution of these movements is the result of wrong methods of teaching. In the first place, one has to realise that the horse has to be engaged for both movements. In order to make sure that the horse will keep stepping with the inner hindleg and that he will lift that hindfoot off the ground, without veering to the outside because of shifting his weight, it is important to begin teaching these movements on the circle. The circle should be about 8 m wide, and the horse should be placed in the travers (haunches-in) position. Great attention must be paid to the movement of the inner hindleg and that the horse keeps the weight on the inside and does not shift to the outside. When the horse has learned to do this, then the circle should become gradually smaller in diameter. The emphasis all the time should be on the stepping of the inner hindleg, and one should be sure that the hindlegs do not fall out of the circle. The French call this "les deux bouts en

93

dedans", "moving with both ends in". Gradually the circle becomes so small that one can speak of a turn on the haunches, and finally it will become a pirouette.

Especially in the canter pirouette one has to take great care that impulsion is maintained. Very often one sees the rider slow down just before asking for the pirouette. If this slowing down is not accompanied by an increase in the driving aids, it is impossible to execute a correct pirouette, because the horse will have lost collection.

According to the rule book, the turn on the haunches can be executed from a halt or from a walk, while the turn on the forehand should be executed from the halt. There is a danger in asking for both these turns from a halt. Most horses lose their engagement when they come to a halt, and one must remember that none of these turns can correctly be executed by a horse without proper engagement.

Those who devote themselves to practice without science are like sailors who put to sea without rudder or compass and who can never be certain where they are going. Practice must always be founded on sound theory

LEONARDO

3 La Guérinière and Shoulder-in

Notwithstanding the fact that in 1983 the F.E.I. decided that shoulder-in should be executed on three tracks, the controversies around this movement will very likely never end. Therefore I think it might be a good idea to go back to the source and find out what la Guérinière really said.

In 1733 François Robichon de la Guérinière published a book called *Ecole de Cavalerie*. Unfortunately, a genius on horseback is not necessarily a master of language; although he is easier to read than any of his predecessors, la Guérinière contradicts himself, causing his illustrator to draw misleading diagrams. As an explanation, I quote Gustave le Bon, a French psychologist, who wrote in his book *L'Equitation Actuelle et ses Principes* (1913): "The fact that the riding masters find it difficult to formulate their methods and contradict themselves can often be explained by the fact that when they ride they use unconsciously their nervous system and when they write they use it consciously."

To understand the aim of la Guérinière when he conceived the idea of shoulder-in, one should read very carefully what he said in explaining how the concept of this movement developed. In the beginning of the chapter on shoulder-in, he states that trotting on a straight line results in only limited suppleness, as it helps the forward movement of the shoulders and legs. The difficulties start when we try to supple the horse so that he can make circles and sideways (lateral) movements.

The Duke of Newcastle wrote endlessly about this problem; he thought that he could solve it by having the horse on the circle with the head in ("la tête dans la volte"). After four chapters about this subject, he writes: ". . . this is the end of my lessons to loosen a horse's shoulders: if you are able to bring these lessons into practice, you can rest assured that you have achieved more than half in schooling a horse."

This was in Chapter XXXI of Newcastle's second book, *La Nouvelle Méthode*, the Chapters XXX, XXXI and XXXII are dedicated to loosening the shoulders. In Chapter XLIV, which deals with how to get the horse on the haunches, he writes: "It is also very true that this, (PUSHING THE HINDQUARTERS OUT IN THE CIRCLE) does not put the horse on the haunches, but very much on the shoulders, (BECAUSE THE PURPOSE OF THIS LESSON IS NOT TO PUT THE HORSE ON THE HIND-QUARTERS THE PURPOSE IS TO LOOSEN THE SHOULDERS)." In this quotation of Newcastle, la Guérinière dropped the words between the brackets, very likely because he knew that no horse can loosen the shoulders when it is on the forehand. In the same Chapter, XLIV, Newcastle writes: ". . . you should press with your inside leg, in order to get the horse's inner hindleg close to the outside hindleg; because of the fact that the hindlegs come under the load and one leg being close to the other it is easy for the horse to keep the hindquarters engaged, NOBODY UNTIL NOW HAS DISCOVERED THIS TRUTH."

All these quotations of the Duke of Newcastle will help the reader to understand the influence Newcastle had on la Guérinière in his search to find a way to loosen the horse's shoulders. Presumably la Guérinière used *La Nouvelle Méthode*. This book was originally written in English in 1667 and in 1677 it was translated by de Solleysel into French. The edition of 1700 was used for the direct quotations.

The two main observations made by Newcastle that guided la Guérinière to the invention of the shoulder-in are: that on the circle the horse comes on the forehand and that when the hindlegs stay close together, the haunches will be engaged. In the quotation that follows it is evident that la Guérinière has done some doctoring in the original text. (The words in capitals are added by la Guérinière.) ". . . the head in, the haunches out, on the circle brings the horse on the forehand . . . (THE SHOULDER CANNOT BECOME SUPPLE) if the inner hindleg does not come close to and in front of the outer hindleg." La Guérinière goes on: "This admission, which experience confirms, makes it very clear that the circle is not the true means to supple the shoulders . . . a profound truth that this illustrious author admits is (THAT THE SHOULDERS CAN

ONLY BE SUPPLED WHEN THE INNER HINDLEG COMES CLOSE TO AND IN FRONT OF THE OUTER HINDLEG) it is this judicious remark that has put me on the way to find the exercise: shoulder-in."

La Guérinière must have been a very modest man to give Newcastle the honour of having written all those words which in reality came from his brain. He substituted *engagement* of the *haunches*, which the Duke was interested in, with *suppling* of the *shoulders*. It is very likely that, because of this, Gustave Steinbrecht in *Das Gymnasium des Pferdes*, suggests that Newcastle was the real inventor of shoulder-in. After having unravelled the texts, I suggest that thanks to the discovery of Newcastle, la Guérinière was able to invent shoulder-in.

The discovery by Newcastle, that the inner hindleg has to come close to the outer hindleg, is of course very important, and, because of the fact that la Guérinière in one paragraph writes that the hindlegs should step over, which has been confirmed by the illustration, riders got in the habit of performing shoulder-in on four tracks (looking at pictures is easier than reading). Until 1983, the F.E.I. rules were not very clear in the description of shoulder-in and the movement became head-in. It was unfortunate that in 1975 shoulder-in became a test movement, together with leg-yielding. The result of all this was that the understanding of the purpose of these two movements got lost. Many riders gave their fantasy a free rein, creating deviations, in which both leg-yielding and shoulder-in lost their identity. A classic example is shoulder-in on the circle; the characteristic of shoulder-in is that in this movement the horse is *not* looking where he is going; therefore doing it on a circle is for me utter nonsense. Evidently these riders got mixed up with the movement: the two ends in (in French "les deux bouts en dedans"). This is an exercise to prepare a horse for the turn on the haunches and the pirouette.

It should be well understood that shoulder-in is one of the basic exercises to develop the skilled movements. Therefore, what has been said in the chapter about leg-yielding, can be repeated for shoulder-in. Variations most of the time become deviations. When that happens, the real purpose of the exercise is not served anymore. Variations as counter shoulder-in, shoulder-in on the diagonal or on the circle infringe on the purpose of shoulder-in as a schooling movement. I am convinced that la Guérinière considered shoulder-in to be a schooling movement because he suggests at the end of the chapter on the renvers the following movements as a sound exercise: shoulder-in in the walk (this is the school walk, mentioned in a later chapter) followed by renvers, then straight on the centre line, alternated by a lively trot.

Now we turn our attention to the execution of the movement shoulder-in. Firstly, it is essential that the horse we plan to teach shoulder-in responds to the pressure of the outside rein against the neck and that he is laterally flexible enough to be able to flex around the rider's inside leg. The rider makes an eight metre circle to prepare the horse. He closes his inside leg, being sure that the leg is just behind the girth, so that the horse will begin to flex around that leg, he also, with his inside hand, vibrates or turns that hand slightly upwards, so that he sees the shimmer of the inside eye. Coming into the straight, the rider tries to keep the flexion, by pushing the shoulders off the track with the outside rein, the hindquarters will stay on the track as long as the rider looks straight in front of himself. The outside leg is passive but ready to prevent the haunches from swinging out. When this happens, the movement becomes leg-yielding and the hindquarters do not push anymore.

One should never forget that the purpose of shoulder-in is to supple the shoulders and to engage the hindquarters. Therefore one should go slowly when teaching this movement to the horse. In the beginning be pleased when the horse tries and maybe performs a shoulder-fore, in which the inner hindleg steps between the two front legs instead of in the track of the outside front leg. After the first try, when the horse has made two or three more or less correct strides, reward the horse and do something different.

Some think that during shoulder-in the body of the horse should make a prescribed angle with the track. I think we should leave geometry out of equitation, because if we are going to look for an angle of a certain amount of degrees, then we overlook the essence of the shoulder-in.

By elevating the shoulder-in to a test movement in 1975, the F.E.I. very likely damaged the concept of shoulder-in, because the riders were worrying more about what the judges wanted to see than about the purpose of shoulder-in.

The violence which accompanies athletics deprives mankind of its intellectual qualities, qualities to which he owes it that he is a man. . . . the pagan worship of the muscle goes directly against what until our days had been the vocation of humanity, that is the passion for comprehension, for intelligence

SOBÈNE OLSTEF

4 Reflections

I would like to reflect upon the state of competitive dressage in its relationship to classical equitation. In order to do this, we have to come to grips with a few basic problems. In the first place, what really is dressage? I think that it is a big word that puts a lot of people off; on the other hand, quite a few people who participate in dressage competition feel themselves far above the crowd.

Instead of "dressage", I would rather use the phrase "schooling the horse", because that is what we really should do when we prepare a horse for the level we want to compete in. The purpose of competition is to find out how far we have advanced in our attempt to prepare a horse for a certain level.

Whatever our ultimate goal may be, eventing, show-jumping, classical dressage or even driving, we have to realise that the basic goal is to help the horse find its balance under the rider. He can only find his balance when he engages his hindquarters, uses his back and becomes supple. In every dressage ride we should see that the horse is engaging (not dragging the hindlegs); we should see that the horse is able to execute the lateral and longitudinal flexions for the level in which he is being presented. The horse should be carrying himself, he should be permeable and he should also be obedient.

When we keep all requisites in mind and then think back upon what we have lately seen, live, on television, or on film, it is not a very rosy picture that comes to mind. To keep the record straight, sometimes there are some surprisingly good exceptions. But only seldom do we see a working trot where the hindquarters are engaged. In the lengthening of the stride or in the extensions, the horse usually loses his balance and falls in two pieces. The transitions are generally too abrupt and lack longitudinal flexion. The turn on the haunches and pirouettes are generally poor, as a result of a lack of lateral flexion and a loss of impulsion. The shoulder-in is most of the time non-existent, because the rider evidently has no clear conception of what the horse is supposed to do during this movement.

At the national level, it is mainly due to poor instruction that the performances are disappointing. It is of course a great privilege to live in a democracy where everybody can say what he wants to. However, as far as equitation is concerned, it would be better if there were more discipline and more humbleness among those teachers with little experience and even less theoretical knowledge.

The basic problem for dressage in America is its youth and consequently it has no doctrine. In Europe there are also difficulties with the coming and going of innovators. But there are always national doctrines to fall back on, when the new theories outlive themselves. The F.E.I. has its troubles; the ground rules are impeccably classical, but the rules that go into details do not always follow the classical concepts.

It was not long after dressage started to expand in America that many Europeans came as instructors. The trouble with this is that they all had different national doctrines. In order to give the reader an idea of what was going on in Europe during the last hundred years, a short history of dressage may be useful here.

Until the Second World War, dressage riding in Europe was mostly influenced by the requirements of military riding. Many of the guiding ideas found their origins in the teachings of de la Guérinière, especially in Germany and in the Austro-Hungarian Monarchy. In France, as a result of the revolution, dressage had a difficult time finding the way back to its classical foundation as developed by the school of Versailles.

In the second half of the 19th century, the French equestrian world was ripped apart by the followers of Antoine d'Aure and François Baucher. The first was a pupil of one of the d'Abzac brothers, who had been "écuyer ordinaire" in Versailles. Although d'Aure developed into a cross-country rider, he never forgot what d'Abzac had taught him. Baucher spent his youth in Milan, Italy, where he became a pupil of Mazzuchelli, a then well-known riding master. Supposedly under the influence of his teacher Baucher developed his famous – for some people infamous – thesis that the will of the horse should be destroyed and the horse should be totally subdued to the will of the rider. He wanted to destroy the instinctive forces, while d'Aure wanted to use these forces. This different approach points to a cultural schism; there are those who

love and those who dominate. Regarding horses, there are
"dresseurs", (trainers – in this context people who school) and
"dompteurs" (tamers). There is no doubt that Baucher has enriched
the hippological vocabulary. He invented the flying change every
stride and he taught his horses to canter on three legs and to canter
backwards. In Vienna, where Baucher gave performances, he was
called the gravedigger of French equitation. Through the influence
of the Duke of Orléans, a son of Louis-Philippe, King of France,
who was at that time president of the cavalry commission, Baucher
was called to Saumur, the military riding school. But when the
duke was killed in an accident shortly after, his brother, the Duke of
Nemours took over the presidency of the commission and not
being an admirer of Baucher, Baucher was asked to leave. Some
time later d'Aure was named "écuyer en chef" at Saumur. Ever
since, Baucher's ideas have had varying influence.

Baucher's influence was at its lowest in the 1930s when General
Decarpentry was president of the dressage commission of the
F.E.I. In this function, he came in close contact with General von
Holzing-Bersted, the President of the F.E.I., also with Gustav Rau
and Ernst Lindenbauer, one of the great Oberbereiter of the
Spanish Riding School. It looked then as if the whole of equestrian
Europe had adopted one doctrine, inspired by de la Guérinière. It
did not last long. After the Second World War, France, presumably
out of chauvinistic reasons, turned back to Baucher. The Swedes,
who used to be followers of the classical German school turned to
Baucher, very likely under the influence of Major St. Cyr, twice
Olympic Gold Medal winner, who had been on detachment in
Saumur.

The classical German school with such names as Steinbrecht, von
Heidebreck, Lörke, Bürkner and Rau, to name a few, has given
way to what I call the neo-German school. In contrast to the
classical German school, this one is purely competition oriented.
From my point of view, Reiner Klimke is the personification of the
neo-German school. Michel Henriquet told me in this connection a
revealing story. When Henriquet visited Klimke in Münster, they
discussed classical dressage. At the end of their conversation,
Klimke said to Henriquet: "You are very likely right, but I ride
dressage competition every weekend and I want to win."

Furthermore, the commentator in *Reiter Revue* of October 1982 had this to say: "The acknowledgement of his phenomenal achievement as a rider does not take away the notion to see in the pair Klimke–Ahlerich from a hippological standpoint a problematic and also a controversial winning combination. As far as his skill in the saddle is considered the new champion is a master without peers, he fails however when one considers the schooling of the horse by means of gymnasticising exercises in order to achieve: pure gaits, a horse without constraints and with collection as the principle goal." To this I want to add that although Klimke was during the Olympic Championships in Los Angeles without any doubt the winner, his presentation, in my opinion, lacked brilliance and did not reach the high standards of classical dressage. Reiner Klimke is a very intelligent and industrious man. Helped by his instinct he has found the weaknesses of the system, which has helped him to reach his goal – winning.

The influence of the Austro–Hungarian school is still traceable today, though since the end of the Second World War we cannot speak of a living Hungarian school any more. After the First World War, the Austro–Hungarian Monarchy was split up. In Vienna the Austrian school lived on, thanks to the Spanish Riding School; in Hungary the traditions of Vienna were continued until the Second World War. From the defunct Austro–Hungarian school there have been very important remnants with influence to this day. For example, Sigmund von Josipovich (1869–1945), instructor at "das Kaiserliche und Königliche Reitlehrer Institut" (school for future military riding instructors) in Vienna until 1914. After the First World War, Josipovich became chief instructor at the Hungarian military riding school, first in Budapest, then Orkeny-Tabor. His pupil Geza von Hazslinszky (1900–80) was also an instructor there. One of his pupils was the man who later should create the American show-jumping style, Bertalan de Nemethy. After having been an instructor at Orkeny-Tabor, Hazslinszky became commander of the Spanish Riding School in Budapest. He was taken prisoner of war by the Russians during the Second World War and sent to Siberia. After his release, the Hungarian communist government made him a csikos (herdsman for horses). Due to the intervention of Prince Bernhard of the Netherlands, then President of the F.E.I., he was set free and allowed to go to the Netherlands. He spent the rest of his life in a position at the Dutch court. Waldemar Seunig and Alois Podhajsky were pupils of Oberbereiter Gottlieb Polak, during their stay at the Spanish Riding School. Furthermore it could be said a number of Germans belong to the Austro–Hungarian school because of their education; Richard Wätjen, who worked twelve years at the Spanish Riding School, Fritz Stecken and Egon von Neindorff, both pupils of Ludwig Zeiner, Bereiter of The Spanish Riding School. Neindorff also worked with Wätjen.

The neo-Germans and the Swedes have the greatest influence as far as dressage riding is concerned in America. However, there are still a few adherents of the classical German and Austro–Hungarian school around. From what I see happening in America, it is evident that a mix of all these different doctrines does not work. The cultural epoch we are living in is not favourable for classical equitation, of which beauty is a fundamental aspect. Modern man is more interested in things mechanical, in acrobatics. But there are still many people who are interested in art for the sake of art, who yearn for what is beautiful. I only partly agree with Egon von Neindorff who said that the adherents of classical dressage are an endangered species. Nothing in history is static; therefore I believe that classical dressage one day will make a comeback.

As far as the international standard is concerned, it seems to me that the inadequacy of many judges, and the complexity of the tests, are to blame for the poor standard of the so-called Grand-dressage. In order to evaluate the standard of international dressage riding in a justifiable way, we have to accept an equitable standard: the standard recognised by the F.E.I. In Chapter I, Article 401, Object and General principles, we read:

Paragraph 1: "The object of Dressage is the harmonious development of the physique and ability of the horse. As a result it makes the horse *calm*, supple, loose and flexible, but also confident, attentive and keen, thus achieving *perfect understanding with his rider*."

Paragraph 2: "These qualities are revealed by: (1) the freedom and regularity of the paces; (2) the harmony, lightness and ease of the movements; (3) the lightness of the forehand and the engagement of the hindquarters, *originating in a lively impulsion*; (4)

the acceptance of the bridle, with light bit contact ('submission throughout' is a wrong translation of 'decontraction totale') and without any tenseness or resistance."

Paragraph 3: "The horse thus gives the impression of doing of his own accord what is required of him. Confident and attentive he submits generously to the control of his rider, remaining absolutely straight in any movements on straight lines and bending accordingly when moving on curved lines."

It is worthwhile pondering these lines and asking ourselves how often have we seen a horse in competition, even at the highest level, who was calm, supple, loose and flexible, with lively impulsion and in understanding with his rider? Or a horse that accepted the bit without tenseness or resistance? How often have we seen movements obtained without apparent effort of the rider as required in Article 417? In the final mark to be given in the Grand Prix test during the 1948 Olympics in London, not only the position and seat of the rider, but also the discretion of the aids applied by the rider had to be evaluated.

Since 1969, having twice visited Wolfsburg, twice Aachen and Goodwood and gone to the Olympic dressage championships in Bromont, Moscow and Los Angeles, and in 1986 the World Championships in Cedar Valley, and also having read the comments about the big meetings by the experts in English, French and German magazines, I cannot say that, measured by the standards given in the F.E.I. rules, what has been presented was very good. Often I have the impression of a downward trend. It seems to me that the main reason for this poor showing lies in the difficulties of the tests. There was a time when one spoke about classical or academic equitation: what we see now looks more like acrobatic equitation. One gets the impression that those who put these tests together do not try to compose a coherent whole, with artistic value. It looks as if they have the preconception that difficulties have to be created, in the same way that the builder of a show-jumping course purposely creates difficulties. The present F.E.I. dressage tests consist of some very difficult movements, strung together one way or another, leaving little room for the grace, beauty and charm that correct dressage should exhibit.

The old Masters tried to create beauty and they knew that they could only achieve this by having a horse that was *really permeable* (durchlässig). As people close to the Renaissance, they pursued the Greek ideal of "kalos k'agathos" (what is beautiful and what is correct). They did not dream of competing with each other by riding a prescribed set of movements within a certain time limit.

At one time I thought that the downward trend could be reversed by trying to make the tests less mechanical with the help of a choreographer. But then I realized that these changes would only be cosmetic and that the cause of the problem is not only that the tests are concatenations of difficult movements, but that the basics should be changed.

I think that everybody involved with classical equitation should ponder the words of Leonardo da Vinci: "Those who devote themselves to practice without science are like sailors who put to sea without rudder or compass and who can never be certain where they are going. Practice must always be founded on sound theory." It is my experience that there is an appalling lack of theoretical knowledge with judges, teachers and consequently with the riders.

The judges should know the rules; they should be the custodians of the equestrian art (Article 418, F.E.I.). The rules of the F.E.I. are the skeleton of the concept that the original authors of those rules had of classical equitation. The hallmarks of these rules are "that the horse gives the impression of doing of his own accord what is required of him" (Article 401.3), and that "all the movements should be obtained without apparent effort of the rider" (Article 417.1). I have the impression that none of the judges ever considers these articles. They are never mentioned at judges' forums. The fact that the riders are concerned about what the judges like to see proves that there is a total misconception of the function of a judge. A judge is the servant of Justitia, the personification of justice. Remember, Justitia is blindfolded so that she is not distracted when she has to decide what is right and what is wrong. No judge can decide about what is right and what is wrong if he does not know the rules.

The teachers should know the theory of equitation so that they understand the purpose of the movements they are teaching and can explain them.

The riders, and for that matter everybody who is involved with horses, should understand that the behaviour of the horse is totally different from that of a human being. Humans think; horses act by instinct. A horse's instinct tells him to flee when he senses danger. The human's approach to this should never be punishment. The horse has an appetence to serve man; man should encourage this by trying to win the horse's confidence. This of course should begin as soon as the foal is born. The daily handling and the grooming are very important stages in the winning of confidence. One should never forget that the horse is an animal that lived originally on wide plains, that he foraged hour after hour while moving. Now he is confined to a straight stall or a 3 m × 3 m box and is being fed a couple of times a day. No wonder that horses get bored and start all kinds of distractions, like crib-biting and weaving.

When Grand Prix riders complain that they have to begin the warm-ups hours before they have to enter the arena, I wonder if they ever do anything else but work their horses in the arena. Felix Bürkner galloped his horses twice a week and Podhajsky used to hunt with his dressage horses until one got damaged and he could not use it any more in competition. What a difference in concept from the lady who said that one should never gallop a dressage horse and always keep it in a small box so that it would not forget collection. All this reinforces my conviction that a new approach is what is needed to save classical equitation.

The judges can influence this change by giving low marks to any performance in which the horse does not give the impression of doing of his own accord what is required of him, and also when the rider shows apparent effort. I am convinced that if the judges become more severe about the position of the rider and of the way in which the rider gives the aids, the overall picture could improve tremendously, because most of the improper executions of the movements are caused by the inadequacies of the rider. It is the rider who fails, not the horse.

We live in a time in which people want to be free, not tied to concepts of olden times. Therefore we see an urgency for innovations, sometimes among very able riders who go overboard and almost become acrobats. We should not forget that art has its own rules and regulations and when we transgress those rules, the art gets lost. Therefore we should not forget the words of Charles

Prosper, Chevalier le Vaillant de Saint Denis: "One must agree that if the true principles of the art had not been maintained, with a certain austerity in the royal riding school in Versailles, if they had not been constantly practised, someday one might be hard-pressed to find the ways to renew the principles."

The poetry of equitation should be reserved for an elite because not everybody can take the road to Corinth

L'HOTTE

5 The Purpose and Structure of Dressage Tests

Before World War II all the competitions in Europe involving horses were exclusively in the hands of the military. They had riding schools, one more famous than the other, where the doctrines of how to school the horses and how to teach the riders were developed. This was logical because a tremendous amount of money was involved to create a staff able to school young untrained horses and to teach the future riders, so that they could become a valuable asset in battle.

Some famous people were involved with the writing of the rules and regulations. In France it was General Alexis l'Hotte, who was responsible for the rules of 1876. In Germany it was Colonel Hans von Heydebreck who was mainly responsible for the rules of 1912.

After the war there were practically no more horses in the armed forces so the civilians had to take over. The national federations realized that the task of guiding the ever increasing masses who had discovered competition on horseback, fell on their shoulders. Realizing the importance of schooling horses in the correct way, dressage tests were composed, becoming progressively more difficult, in which the riders were asked, at different levels of difficulty to show that they had correctly gymnasticized and suppled the horse for the level pertinent to the progress the horse had made.

One can compare these progressive exercises with those musicians and ballet dancers practise in order to develop the skills that will enable them to perform the works of great composers or choreographers. The pianist has to practise the scales to get perfect control of his fingers, the singer has to get control over his voice, and the dancer, from an early age on, has to spend hours at the barre to gain perfect control over his body.

As far as I know it is only Karl Czerny who has composed studies for the piano incorporating the skill-developing exercises. This is not music for the concert hall, but it is less boring than playing scales.

The flawless execution of the concerto or the ballet is the result of the perfectly developed skills. The concerto or for that matter the ballet are primarily works of art because the composer or choreographer were inspired. The executors create a work of art because they put their soul into their performance and because they have mastered the needed skills.

In dressage competition we have never come out of the skill-developing movements. The Grand Prix has become a concatenation of very difficult movements, all demonstrating the acquired skills, making it impossible for the rider–horse combination to perform equestrian art and for the judges to get an impression of the whole. This is the reason that I speak of acrobatic equitation. When one difficult movement follows the other, there is no more rhythm in the performance and without rhythm there is no art. Let us not forget that the F.E.I. instituted an International Dressage Event to preserve the *art*. Very seldom, and never at the highest levels, does one see a horse–rider combination in which the horse gives the impression of doing of his own accord what the rider asks of him, where the rider gives aids that are invisible to the eye of the beholder, and where one gets the impression that horse and rider are one. When these artistic performances are seen, spectators will say: "That was beautiful."

The Kur could have been the revival of the equestrian art. A programme composed by the rider or somebody else, free of compulsory movements, so that the composers could give their inspiration free rein. Unfortunately the F.E.I., afraid that the performances might turn into a circus, introduced compulsory movements, thereby taking away the freedom without which art is impossible. It seems that Article 420.4 is a guarantee against any circus influences: "The test includes all the school paces and all the fundamental airs of Classical High School, of which the fancy paces, based on extreme extension of the forelegs, are no part. For this reason, the school leaps, obsolete in a great many countries, do not figure in the test."

If the rules remain as strict as they are now, with all those boring compulsory movements in the Freestyle, we shall get the same succession of the skill-developing movements. There may be a rider or choreographer with an artistic approach, who may put some artistry in the programme, but it will be comparable with the studies of Czerny, that never became concert music.

To attain the summit in dressage, a rider has to be intelligent and mature; in addition he must have enormous powers of empathy. It is this last attribute in particular that enables the gifted rider to breathe a stirring artistic quality into a merely technically correct presentation.

ALBRECHT

The Roots of
Classical Equitation

Classical equitation is, in German, *Klassische Reitkunst*, mostly used in the Germanic and English languages. The French speak generally about "équitation académique" and "équitation artistique". "Equitation classique" is the French equivalent of classical equitation. The only time I found this expression, was in the title of a book published by André Gérard in 1974 namely: *Les Maîtres de l'Equitation Classique*. The book begins with a complete reproduction of the second part of *Ecole de Cavalerie*, by la Guérinière, and by a selection of epitomes of writings by authors who were strongly influenced by la Guérinière. Michel Henriquet made the choices. In his introduction the publisher, Gérard, notes that this selection was made because of the value they represent for the modern rider. What is significant for what follows later in this chapter is that Gérard calls *Ecole de Cavalerie* a fundamental text.

Until Louis XIV opened his stables in Versailles in 1682, most riding was goal-oriented. Horses had to be schooled for war, transportation, hunting and sundry domestic uses. In Versailles, it was the "écuyers cavalcadours" who had to take care of the schooling of the King's horses. But the "écuyers ordinaires" were under no pressure since the King paid for everything. The most talented of them, realizing that one could make the horse do some very beautiful things, developed riding to all its glory. This became known as the School of Versailles. The names of these great riders are known, but they did not write.

It was François Robichon de la Guérinière (1688–1751), Ecuyer du Roi from 1715, who was able, guided by what the "écuyers" of Versailles had achieved in creating real equestrian art, to put all this together in his book *Ecole de Cavalerie*, 1731. He was never a part of the School of Versailles, but his teacher, Antoine de Vendeuil, was at one time "écuyer ordinaire". Because of la Guérinière's great reputation as a rider and as a teacher he was, in 1730, allowed to found an academy of his own in the former royal stables in the Tuileries. His fame spread all over Europe and many young noblemen came to him to be instructed. In 1791 a German translation of *Ecole de Cavalerie* was published. The result of all this was that, in the Spanish Riding School in Vienna, this book was considered to be the Bible of the equestrian art. According to Podhajsky, this was owing to the influence of one of the most famous Oberbereiter, Max Ritter von Weyrother, who served the Spanish Riding School from 1813 to 1833; as Oberbereiter from 1825.

Maybe it is far-fetched, but I would not be surprised if this was the reason why the doctrine of the Spanish Riding School, being based on la Guérinière, became known as classical equitation ("Klassische Reitkunst"). Podhajsky called the Spanish Riding School "The last conservatory of Classical Equitation" ("die letste Pflegestelle Klassischer Reitkunst"). Therefore, I consider equitation to be classical if it is founded on the School of Versailles, as interpreted by la Guérinière. This does not mean that the system is closed, as long as the basic principles are adhered to, there is nothing against expanding the system. La Guérinière never described the extensions or the flying changes. Now these movements are all asked for in the higher level tests, and rightly so, because these movements are an integral part of the beauty of classical equitation.

I think that Steinbrecht and l'Hotte are also to be considered as contributors to Classical Equitation because they both, independently and in their own language, claimed that the horse should go forward and be straight.

One thing has, as far as I know, been systematically overlooked, namely that la Guérinière never mentions the trot in connection with the shoulder-in. In the chapter about haunches-in he suggests that it is a good exercise in the beginning of a lesson to ask the horse to proceed in shoulder-in, in the walk ("au pas").

In *Plaisirs Equestres* No 157, Serge Beylier explains that the reason for this is that in the 17th and 18th centuries there was a difference between the "pas de campagne" and the "pas d'ecole" (the ordinary walk and the school walk). The latter was a diagonal walk, a movement easily performed by the Iberian horses who in those times were the preferred horses for school work. After reading the article by Beylier, I realized that this was the reason why the Duke of Newcastle, in both his books, states that the movement of the walk is the same as the movement of the trot. I always thought that this statement was proof of the Duke's shortsightedness and I was amazed that this mistake had been perpetuated by de Solleysel, his translator. How wrong I have been.

This also explains why de Lubersac was able, after having schooled his horses only in the walk for 18 months to two years, to produce horses who were proficient in all gaits and able to execute the most difficult movements. He schooled the horses in the school walk.

Now it is a major mistake if a horse shows a diagonal walk. But let us not forget that the piaffe is a diagonal movement, as is the rein-back. (More on the reason why the diagonal walk became obsolete in a following chapter.)

Ride your horse forward and make it go straight

STEINBRECHT

Quiet, forward, straight

L'HOTTE

7 Why and When the Diagonal Walk Became Obsolete

At the end of the first chapter of the second part of *Ecole de Cavalerie*, la Guérinière stated that theory is necessary in order to school any horse correctly, whether for the cavalry, for the hunt, or for the school, so that the rider can be comfortable because his mount has been suppled, made obedient and has learned to engage the hindquarters.

In the fifth chapter, la Guérinière deals with the natural gaits of a horse. In Article 1 of that chapter, when writing about the walk, he claims that it is the least elevated movement, the slowest and the most easy of all gaits for the rider. He also describes the walk as a four-beat movement. Amazingly the etching presenting this walk shows very clearly the diagonal walk.

At the end of the ninth chapter, la Guérinière writes: "There are two kinds of walk, the normal walk and the school walk." He does not mention that the school walk is a diagonal movement, but he says that it is a lofty, shortened and collected movement.

Perhaps a historical perspective will help in understanding how this diagonal walk became obsolete. During the time that artistic equitation (the term classical equitation was coined in the middle of the 1800s), reigned supreme in Versailles, there existed a lot of private riding academies all over France. La Guérinière had one such school. In 1715 he started an academy in Paris, it became such a resounding success, that in 1730, Prince Charles of Lorraine, "grand ecuyer", reopened the stables of the Tuileries for his "protégé", they had been closed when, in 1680, the royal stables were moved to Versailles.

There also existed a number of military riding schools. Most of the instructors had been in Versailles, but they realized that, at the military riding schools, they had to develop a different doctrine of equitation; a doctrine geared to the requirements demanded of a cavalry horse. Drummond de Melfort (1722–1788) who had spent some time in Prussia to study the tactics of Frederic II, King of Prussia, wrote: "We have to give up a beautiful position on the horse and everything that is delicate, grace and perfection", and d'Auvergne thought that "all the brilliance of artistic equitation had no purpose; that which is useful and efficient surpassed all what to him were superfluities." D'Auvergne was in charge of the first French Military Riding School, he did not write, but had a spokesman in Boisdeffre (1747–1827).

The debacle at Rossbach, where in 1757 the French cavalry was routed by the Prussians proved that the convictions of these men were correct. In 1766 the first French Cavalry manual was issued, formulating the new doctrine.

Versailles was closed in 1789 as a result of the outbreak of the French Revolution. The former attendants of the "écuyers" stayed and took over the riding instruction of the cadre, teaching, first the revolutionary army, and then the army of Napoleon. They understood that they had to teach the opposite of the dogma they had once been taught. Now they emphasized stretched and free movements of the horse and not collection or the exaggerated engagement of the haunches. Evidently they had understood what l'Hotte more than 100 years later formulated in this way, "Instruction has to be conceived and executed so that it can achieve the anticipated goals, and so that those to whom the instruction is given have the opportunity to achieve the goals."

During the restoration of the monarchy, there was a short revival of the School of Versailles, but it never had the appeal of before, the interest had changed from artistic riding to outdoor riding. In 1830, Versailles was closed for good.

Since there was no place for the diagonal walk in military riding nor in any outdoor riding, it is easy to understand why the diagonal, or the school walk, found its end at the beginning of the French Revolution.

Pignatelli, convinced by his own experience that the function of the bit is rather to let the horse know what the rider wants than to constrain the horse, said that if the bits had of their own the miraculous quality to make the mouth of the horse and to make the horse obedient, both rider and horse would be all set after a visit to the tack shop

LA GUÉRINIÈRE

8 Contact or No Contact

There seems to be an occasional controversy between those who claim that it is necessary to have contact with the horse's mouth and those who claim that this is not necessarily the case.

When we pursue the schooling of a horse from the very beginning to the highest level, artistic equitation, then we will understand that, during this endeavour, there are different gradations in the amount of contact the rider has with the horse. I think that it is very dangerous to speak about "no contact" when those whom we address have very little experience. On the other hand, a horse can be ruined by too heavy a hand, especially in the walk.

The discussions in the German Cavalry Manual of 1912 on the working trot and the working canter are very explicit about the walk: "As far as the walk is concerned, greatest attention should be given to the creation and maintenance of a correct and pure walk; therefore premature and strong resistance with the reins should be avoided. An incorrect, uneven and dragging walk will improve most of the time after the horse has learned to trot properly."

Young horses should be helped to accept the bit after having been accustomed to the snaffle on the lunge line. The rider should try to achieve very light and elastic contact. The young horse should never have the feeling of being constrained. Constraint would not only cause resistances, but also would impede the forward movement of the horse, especially in the walk.

If one rides with elastic contact, following the movement of the horse, every horse will stretch the neck and decontract the moment that the rider opens the hands and lets the reins slide through the fingers (this is not quite the equivalent of the German: "aus der Hand kauen lassen"). This sliding can of course only happen with flat, smooth reins.

Why do we want contact? Because we want to communicate with the horse; we want to shorten and to lengthen the frame of the horse and we want to improve the lateral flexibility. In other words, we want the horse to become permeable (French: "perméable", German: "durchlässig"). This means that the horse lets the impulsion, created by the driving aids of the rider, go from the hindquarters through the back and the neck muscles, causing flexion of the poll and causing the horse to accept the bit, without stiffening of the jaw. The acceptance of the bit means that the driving aids and the guiding aids have met. At this point the process reverses itself: the guiding aids regulating the impulsion, taking care of the longitudinal and the lateral flexions and also of the different gaits and movements. One of the most important and most difficult things in classical equitation is to have *elastic* contact. I think that the question is not *contact* or *no contact*, but the *quality* of the contact. Therefore I believe that as soon as the beginner rider has found some balance on the horse while being lunged, he should be instructed right away how to develop an elastic contact. In the first place, he should learn not to use his arm muscles but his back muscles. Furthermore, he should develop an elastic contact by never having a stretched elbow joint but a flexible one which opens and closes. The best way to teach this is on a horse that has a good walk. The rider while keeping the reins straight all the time, with the lightest contact, should learn to follow the movements of the horse's head. A horse will fight the rider's hand if constrained by the rider using his arm muscles and by not having elastic contact. As I put it, the rider puts on the hand-brake.

I compare the reins with the strings of a violin. There has to be tension in the strings so that a tone develops. There has to be tension in the reins so that the rider can communicate with the horse. Mild tension produces a low tone in the string, as the tension increases the tone becomes higher. Transferring this to the reins, there should always be a steady tone. A low tone is analogous to a light contact. If there are loops in the reins there is no even, steady tone, this means that the rider does not have an elastic contact. However, when the rider vibrates with the inside hand in order to see the shimmer of the inside eye, then there is evidently no steady tone. It is also evident that the tone of both reins is not always the same.

During the schooling period, in which we want the horse to come under with the hindquarters, there will be times that we need to apply a lot of contact. At this time, the horse has to learn that when we create more impulsion and increase the resistance, he should not try to go faster and become longer, but he should try to get his hindquarters under his body. Once the horse has learned to do this, he will carry himself. The more he carries himself, and the more he understands what the rider wants from him, the lighter the contact will become. The experienced rider responds to this by decreasing the tightness of the hands. One might say that the rider should let his hands breathe. One could call this "descente de main".

No contact is an ideal that only very few people attain. I have known perhaps five people who have achieved this unity with the horse. It is distressing to say, but I have never seen it in competition, not even in Grand Prix or in the Kur.

I hope that the reader will understand that the above is strictly for classical equitation. Other forms of equitation such as Western have totally different objects. Because the Western rider has to have his hands free for roping, he does not want his horse to accept the bit. He is not interested in longitudinal, or lateral flexions. He neckreins and makes sliding halts by putting on the hand-brake. By using very sharp bits he achieves this goal.

In the world of nomadic horse breeders the lifestyle of the rider points to a way of life of higher values in which the horse is not only looked upon as a means for livelihood, or transportation, or battle, but rather as the embodiment of this higher lifestyle

JANKOVICH

The Kur

The musical Freestyle, the Kur, is the opportunity the rider has to show classical equitation in all its beauty. The A.H.S.A. recognizes three levels: the fourth level, the Intermediate I and the Grand Prix.

What I miss in the rules concerning the Freestyle is that there is no mention being made of qualifying for a Freestyle ride. I think that it is very important that all the participants should have proven that they and their horses are proficient in their chosen level. For example, in order to enter an Intermediate I Freestyle the rider should have at least three scores of over 60 per cent in Intermediate competitions, in order to qualify.

Furthermore the Kur should not only be artistic but also technically impeccable. The programme on paper may be beautiful but if the rider is not able to execute the more difficult movements adequately, he or she should be eliminated.

Sometimes one sees riders who begin their Kur programme with piaffe and passage. From a choreographic standpoint this is wrong, a programme should evolve to a climax, there should be a certain rhythm in a programme; when the climax comes right at the beginning, one can only go down. It is of course worse when the horse gets his legs barely off the ground and when it is the rider who makes all kinds of body movements, hoping that this perhaps may convince the horse to try a piaffe. In Vienna the audience boos a singer off the stage if he cannot stay on key.

Another problem with the Kur is the music. There are different opinions about what the function of music during a Kur really is. During the performances of the Spanish Riding School the music is mainly background. In *l'Année Hippique* 1985/86 Gabriela Grillo wrote an article about the musical Kur. Grillo is a graduate musicologist who was for many years the German Kur specialist. In the article she decribes the festivities in the 17th century involving horses. These festivities evolved to what was then and still is called carousel.

Grillo writes about a dance on horseback in which the horse

evidently did the dancing. She claims that for these carousels music was of great importance, not only as an illustration of the performance but also as a decisive element of the choreography. Unfortunately Grillo does not mention any composers of this kind of music and since I have never heard it, it is impossible to evaluate.

I think that classical equitation should be accompanied by classical music. The music should be festive, not a farce. Vocal music is inappropriate, and a speech or address by the rider should entail elimination.

For many years both figure-skating and ice-dancing have been accompanied by music. Unfortunately the way the skaters incorporate the music has been taken as an example by many riders. I do not think that what the horse–rider combination does can be compared with what the skater does. I also think that it is unfortunate to talk about dancing horses. Of course when a horse moves energetically with a swinging back the rider can get the feeling that the horse is dancing under him, but we should never forget that we use the expression "dancing" metaphorically.

Those who follow the lead of the ice-skaters think that the music should accompany the ride and have the same beat as the movements of the horse. This results most of the time in the editing of different compositions, in order to provide the beat of the trot or the canter. Generally speaking such editing is an artistic failure. Since the walk is a movement without any impulsion, it is very difficult to find fitting music. On top of this, the walk, the turn on the haunches and rein-back are such boring movements that I think they should never be included in a Kur programme.

The Kur was made part of the World Cup because it had become clear that the Grand Prix tests were so boring that they hardly attracted any spectators. Since the World Cup is big business and money had to be made, the organizers thought the Kur might attract the masses. Notwithstanding the fact that the F.E.I. has, because of the compulsory movements, made it impossible for the riders to display equestrian art, the public has come, because they see the Kur as a circus where they can boo if they do not agree with the judging. It is degrading for the equestrian art that the public thinks it has the knowledge to judge what has been presented.

The F.E.I. hesitated to accept the Kur, because of the possibility that it would become a circus. I am afraid it has become a circus, not so much because of what the riders present but rather because of the atmosphere that has been created around the World Cup. Although I am a firm believer in the idea of the Kur, I regret that the F.E.I. ever accepted it.

Glossary

A.H.S.A.	American Horse Show Association.
Corinth	"not everybody is allowed to go to Corinth." There are two interpretations of this old Greek saying.
	1) The harbour of Corinth was very difficult to enter, therefore only a skilled sailor could do this.
	2) Corinth at one time was a very wealthy community with rather loose morals. When Demosthenes asked a famous courtesan by the name of Lais what the price for her favours was, she asked ten thousand drachmas. According to the story Demosthenes turned away, remarking: "I will not buy regret by such a price." In other words Corinth was too expensive for ordinary people.
Ecuyer	Originally the bearer of the écu, the shield.
Ecuyer en Chef	First Rider and Director of the former military Riding School in Saumur, France.
Ecuyer cavalcadour	See Index Nominum, Versailles.
Ecuyer ordinaire	See Index Nominum, Versailles.
F.E.I.	Federation Equestre International (International Equestrian Federation).
Gymnastic	Pertaining to physical exercises that develop strength and agility.
Gymnastics	The practice or art of gymnastic exercises.
Gymnastically	Adverb of above.
Exercises, loosening	To loosen or supple the muscles.
Exercises, collecting	To stimulate the flexing of the muscles.
Exercises, gymnastic	To develop the tone and strength of the muscles.
Tone	That state of the body or of an organ in which all its functions are performed with healthy vigour.

Gymnasticise	To make a horse perform those exercises that will enhance the horse to function with healthy vigour.
Manipulate	To work skilfully with the hands.
Marshall	OHG marahscalh, marah (horse), scalh (servant).
Permeable	The literal translation of the German expression "Durchlässig", meaning "letting through". A horse is permeable when it lets the impulsion, created by the driving aids of the rider, go from the hindquarters through the back and the neck muscles, causing flexion of the poll and causing the horse to accept the bit, without stiffening of the jaw. The acceptance of the bit means that the driving aids and the guiding aids have met. At this point the process reverses itself, the guiding aids regulating the impulsion, taking care of the longitudinal and lateral flexions and also of the different gaits and movements.

Index Nominum

Academy

According to Lilly Powell-Froisard, *Plaisirs Équestres* #121, we have to trace the origins of the Academies during the flourishing of the Renaissance in Italy. The Greek ideal of education, the body in harmony with the mind, received new life through the rediscovery of the Greek classics. All over Italy, Academies for young noblemen were set up. The curriculum included: Greek, Latin, painting, music, mathematics, astronomy, dance, fencing and equitation.

Evidently people like Grisone, Fiaschi, Pignatelli, Pluvinel and others had to set up these elaborate schools in order to get pupils. Or maybe some of them were just members of the staff.

Alexander Technique

Frederick Matthias Alexander was born in Tasmania in 1869; he died in 1955. His ambition was to become a singer and reciter; in the process he lost his voice. Not getting any help from the medical profession, he tried to find out for himself what was wrong. Looking in a mirror he saw that he tightened muscles around his throat. Out of this insight, Alexander developed a technique whereby a person can develop a good posture and gain complete control over his body, without becoming rigid.

Auvergne, Jacques, Amable d' (1729–98)

He entered the military service in 1744, with the "chevauxlegérs de la maison du roi". His first instructor was François de Lubersac, "écuyer cavalcadour" in 1736 and "écuyer ordinaire" in 1740. In 1750, Drummond de Melfort joined the chevauxlegérs. Lubersac was pure School of Versailles, while Drummond de Melfort was educated on the battlefields. It is there that he learned that the school movements taught at Versailles had no place in military riding. The cruel confirmation of his conviction was the outcome of the battle of Rossbach where, in 1757, the French cavalry was routed by the Prussians, under Seydlitz. In 1756, at 27, d'Auvergne was called to be the "écuyer en chef" of the École Militaire in Paris. (One of his pupils there was Napoleon.) D'Auvergne never published any books. However, some of his pupils, Bohan, Boisdeffre and de Chabannes quoted d'Auvergne extensively in their writings. For example, he objected to collected gaits, the balance on the hindquarters, and he stressed forward movements in a horizontal balance.

Baucher, François (1796–1873)

Born in Versailles, Baucher was sent, when he was 14, to his uncle in Milan, who was equerry to Prince Borghese, husband of Napoleon's sister, Pauline. From his later writings, it is evident that he came strongly under the influence of Mazzuchelli. In 1816, Baucher went back to France to work in riding schools in le Havre and Rouen. In 1834, he went to Paris to run a riding school with J. Ch. Pellier. In 1837, he joined the circus of Laurent and Adolphe Franconi. He did this to be able to show his interpretation of riding as laid down in his first book, *Dictionnaire raisonné d'Équitation* (1833). In that age, the circus was the gathering point for society. Baucher introduced himself as a renovator and claimed that before him nobody had ever really understood the essence of equitation. He showed: halt on three legs, trot backwards, change of lead every other stride, pirouettes in the canter on three legs, canter backwards. His performance caused quite a bit of commotion. His admirers consisted of The Duke of Orléans, Lord Seymour, Lamartine, Delacroix and Théophile Gauthier, while his antagonists counted among them the Duke de Nemours, Alexandre Dumas, George Sand and Gustave Flaubert. It is quite interesting to note that the world of letters took such a keen interest in what happened in a circus. In 1842 Baucher's main book, *Méthode d'Équitation*, was first published. It has become known as the "first method". Faverot de Kerbrech revised the text and added to it in 1874. This is known as the "second method". The aim of dressage as expounded in the first method is to break the will of the horse and to shape it into a docile instrument of the rider. Much was done standing still, severe bits were used and sharp spurs were not spared. In 1855 Baucher had a crippling accident when a heavy chandelier fell on him. This accident and the mellowing that comes with age brought the second method, in which the horse is schooled in motion. Less stress is put on the spurs and the advantage of the snaffle is put forward.

Bourgelat, Claude (1712–79)

He was born in Lyon, France and was educated by the Jesuits. For a quarter of a century he managed the Riding Academy of Lyon. There is a story that he studied law in Toulouse and practiced law in Grenoble. He also may have served in the cavalry, in a troop of the King's Musqueteers. In 1740 he was called to manage the Riding Academy. In 1744 he published his first and only book on equitation *Le Nouveau Newcastle, ou Nouveau Traité de cavalerie géometrique, théorique et pratique*. This was later to be followed by many publications on veterinary subjects. For many years, books have been written dealing with veterinary science and equitation. Originally, the emphasis was on the veterinary part, but later the emphasis shifted to the equitational part; in Bourgelat's case the change went to the veterinary. In 1762 he founded the first Veterinary School at Lyon. At the request of Louis XV, he founded the second Veterinary School at Alfort, just outside Paris.

Duarte, King of Portugal (1401–38)

He became king in 1433 but died in 1438, a victim of the plague. There exists a manuscript of his dated 1434 of which the title is: "The book to teach to ride well in all saddles". In the Iberian Peninsula, as a result of the Moorish occupation, during about six centuries, the Iberians had to adapt themselves to the ways the Moors fought in order to fight them successfully. The Moors rode a lighter horse, fast and manoeuvrable, against which the heavy western European horses had no chance. The Iberians also, after they had started to use the light type horses, adapted to the way the Moors rode and used short stirrups, with a high saddle. This was called riding *a la gineta*. This makes it clear that the Iberians had to be able to ride in two saddles. The manuscript of Duarte's book, for some reason, was found in the National Library in Paris. In 1842 the first Portugese edition was published in Paris and the second one in 1843 in Lisbon. There exists a fragmentary translation into French by Bacharach, published in *L'Année Hippique*, 1959. There is not a trace of cruelty in Duarte's writings; he evidently was a real *dresseur* and not a *dompteur*. Monteilhet, in *Les Maîtres de l'Oeuvre équestre*, ranks him between Xenophon and Pluvinel.

Fiaschi, Césare, (15(?)–75)

When Griso had his school in Naples, Fiaschi had his in Ferrara, probably about 1539. He wrote a book in 1556, dealing with subjects such as: "How to handle and how to bit horses and how to shoe them". This last part is considered to be excellent, while the other parts rank even with Griso's theories. Fiaschi introduced music during riding, because he believed that without music and rhythm nothing good can happen.

Glahn, Erich (1879–1960)

Glahn was a staunch defender of the purity of the principles of classical equitation. He was a frequent contributor to *Sankt Georg* and wrote *Die Reitkunst am Scheideweg* and *Die Weltreiterei und Wir*, as well as a few novels. Seunig considers him to be the successor of von Heydebreck and von Josipovich as advocate of classical equitation.

Grisone, Federigo (16th century)

His book, *Gli Ordini di Cavalcare*, was published in 1555. Grisone was a pupil of Colas Pagano, the son of the "écuyer en chef" of the King of Naples, D. Ferranto, the illegitimate son of the King of Aragon. This could mean that there was Spanish influence in Pagano's teaching. Since *Gli Ordini di Cavalcare* was the first book on riding ever to be published in Italian, it found a wide audience. It was translated into French in 1559 and into German in 1570. As happens so often, the bad things make more impression than the good things. And there certainly are a lot of bad things in this book. But after studying it carefully, it remains in one's memory as a mixture of great kindness and ruthless brutality.

A French critic had this to say: "He has, as many modern riders, sensed the theory, without knowing the theory." The same critic calls him a rider without peer.

von Heydebreck, Hans (1866–1935)

He was an acknowledged expert in equitation and wrote several books and aricles. Co-author of the German cavalry manual of 1912. Commentator of Steinbrecht's *Gymnasium des Pferdes*.

l'Hotte, Alexis Francois (1825–1905)

Friend and pupil of both Baucher and d'Aure (1798–1863). D'Aure was a pupil of the School of Versailles after the Restoration. He believed in a forward moving horse and strongly attacked Baucher. L'Hotte was able to bring the two opposed methods into a synthesis, proscribing, however, the extravagances of Baucher. He was in Saumur as "Écuyer" (1860–64), "Écuyer en chef" (1864–70), and as a general commanding officer of the whole of Saumur (1874–79). He wrote two famous books, *Questions Équestres* and *Officier de Cavalerie*.

von Josipovich, Sigmund (1869–1945)

He worked together with von Heydebreck and was Instructor at K.u.K. Militär Reitlehrer Institut in Vienna. He had great influence on the development of classical equitation in Austria and Hungary.

La Broue, Salomon de (c. 1530–c. 1610)

A pupil of Pignatelli, he wrote the first book on riding in the French language (1593). His second book, *Le Cavalerice françois*, which appeared in 1610, had a great impact. He differed from de Pluvinel in that he emphasised work in the exterior; he introduced what we now call cavalletti. He is also the first to ask for flexion in the poll. He stresses lightness: "The lightness of the mouth of the horse precedes the lightness of the horse." After he came back from Italy, he was for some time "écuyer ordinaire de la Grande Écurie du roi", to Henri IV.

La Guérinière, François Robichon de (1688–1751)

He was born in Essay, a small town near Alençon, where his father was a lawyer; he also was an officer at the court of the Duchess of Orléans. In 1715, he received his title as "écuyer du roi", which entitled him to give lessons. He never had a function at the palace in Versailles. He was a pupil of Antoine de Vendeuil, who at one time was "écuyer ordinaire" in Versailles. In 1730, Prince Charles of Lorraine, "grand écuyer de France" (master of the horse) named him director of the Manége at the Tuileries. Notwithstanding the fact that his reputation as an extraordinary teacher had become international and that he received pupils from all over Europe, he was most of the time in financial trouble. Evidently La Guérinière was not a good businessman. In 1731, he published his book, *École de cavalerie*. In contrast to most of his predecessors, La Guérinière was evidently a very methodical man. While La Broue, Pluvinel and the Duke of Newcastle ramble along and are very repetitious, la Guérinière has a strict scheme and stays with it. (Maybe it was because his father was a lawyer.) What contributed mostly to La Guérinière's fame was the fact that he invented the shoulder-in.

Newcastle, William Cavendish, Duke of (1592–1676)

William Cavendish was a man of great wealth; his grandfather had been Treasurer both to Henri VIII and Edward VI. He was a staunch supporter of Charles I in his fights with the Scots and with the Long Parlement. He helped the king out with £10,000 to raise an army, the treasury being empty and the king without an army. Later he raised an army for himself to help the king fight the Long Parlement. As a reward, he was allowed to mint money and to confer knighthood. At Marston Moor, however, he was defeated in 1644 and had to flee England. Via Rotterdam he arrived in Paris where he married a young lady in waiting to Queen Henriette and went from there to Antwerp, where he found lodging with the widow of Rubens, the famous painter. He started a riding school in Antwerp and operated it for 18 years. He wrote his first book in Antwerp, and he had the good fortune to find an excellent engraver, a former pupil of Rubens, to illustrate the book, Abraham van Diepenbeke, a Dutch painter, born *c.* 1607 in Bois-le-Duc. Originally a glazier, he gave this up because of the fire hazards. A prolific producer, he was very much in demand by book publishers to make vignettes and illustrations. In 1660, with the restoration of Charles II, the Duke went back to England. He retired from public life and lived alternately on his estates Welbeck and Bolsover. At this time, he wrote a second book. In a preface, he makes it clear that this second book is not a translation of the first (this one having been published in French) neither an expansion, but a new book because of new insights. After a bad translation into French by somebody who did not know anything about horses, Jacques de Solleysel, "écuyer de la Grande Écurie", made an excellent translation.

The illustrations in the book are beautiful, the text is very repetitious, the contents are controversial, and the Duke is an extremely vain man: according to him his method has never been thought of before; his ways are marvellous and nobody ever thought of them before; the authors who wrote before him did not understand anything about equitation. But he was an extremely faithful servant to his king.

Pignatelli, Giambattista (16th century)

Very likely born around 1525, he died presumably before the end of the century. He was a pupil of Fiaschi. There are no writings left of Pignatelli (however, there should be some manuscripts of him around somewhere). Pignatelli was a rider and teacher of great fame and he has had an everlasting influence on the development of equitation in Europe. Four of his most distinguished pupils were Salomon de la Broue (1552–1602), Antoine de Pluvinel (1555–1620), de St. Antoine, whom Henri II sent to Queen Elizabeth, and Georg Engelhard Löhneysen Della Cavalleria (1588) who brought equitation to Germany.

Pluvinel, Antoine de (1555–1620)

At age ten, he was sent to Italy where he studied under Pignatelli. At the riding academies in those years the pupils received a complete education. Back in France, he was attached to the court of the brother of King Charles IX, the Duke of Anjou. In 1573, this duke was elected King of Poland, and Pluvinel accompanied him to his new kingdom. When, in 1574, his brother Charles IX died, the Duke decided to give up the throne of Poland and to go back to France. He fled from Poland with three French noblemen, one of which was Pluvinel; they rode non-stop from Cracow to Paris. In 1589 Henri IV succeeded to the throne of France at the death of Henry III. Pluvinel kept all his charges under the new king: chamberlain, tutor of the dauphin (later Louis XIII) and of the Duke of Vendome. In 1594 Pluvinel was licensed to open a riding academy in Paris. It seems that as a young man, the Cardinal de Richelieu was a pupil at Pluvinel's academy. In 1609 he was sent as ambassador to the Netherlands, where he met Crispyn de Pas, Jr. who was an engraver in Utrecht. Thanks to this meeting we have the most beautiful engravings of any book on horses. I think that de Pluvinel's fame was mostly due to these engravings. Pluvinel took notes, on the orders of the king, whenever he gave lessons to the king (Louis XIII had been his pupil when he still was dauphin). Pluvinel had given those notes to his friend Menou de Charnizay to safeguard them, hoping that later he would be able to use them in order to make a book. However, Pluvinel died before he had even started to order the notes. Crispyn de Pas, who had practically finished the etchings, got hold of a friend of his, a servant of Pluvinel, by the name of Peyrol, who managed to get him a collection of discarded notes. Since de Pas was short of money he published his etchings, badly annotated, on his own in 1623. When Menou de Charnizay found out what had happened, he went to the king and asked the permission to publish the book with a text he, Charnizay, would take care *of at the hand of the* notes. The result was two books, the first one published by de Pas with beautiful etchings under the name *Manége Royale*, and a second one published by Menou de Charnizay with the authentic text, but with bad illustrations, under the name *Instruction du Roy* (1625). Because of the etchings of de Pas, later also used for the editions prepared by Charnizay, the book of Pluvinel received a great approval, more so than that of Salomon de la Broue, which was published in 1602. I think we can learn more from de la Broue, but his book did not have the beautiful pictures.

Rousselet, Jean (1783–1858)

After having taken part in most of the Napoleonic campaigns in Germany, Poland, Spain, Portugal and Russia, he received, in 1814, an appointment as instructor in Saumur. He had the reputation of being very kind with his horses; as one admirer said: "He spoke the language of the horses", and of being very patient with his pupils. He retired in 1849.

Seunig, Waldemar (1887–1976)

He was born in Laibach, Duchy of Krain, in the former Donau Monarchy. He was a descendant of traders and craftsmen who at the instigation of Maria-Theresia, Queen of Hungary, had emigrated to what is now Slowenia. The Seunigs developed into well-to-do landowning merchants in the town that is now called Llubljana.

After three years of Officers School in Wiener-Neustadt, Austria, he entered the cavalry in a Uhlan Regiment. First he was in Lemberg; then he went, after a few years to Olmütz, Moravia. In about 1911 he was sent to K. und K. Reitlehrer Institut, the imperial and royal School for future military riding instructors, in Vienna. There he became the pupil of Josipovich who would have a great influence on him. After four years of war on the Russian and Italian front, the government in Vienna told him to go to the country where he was born, Krain, and find something for himself. By that time, Krain had become part of Yugoslavia under the name of Slowenia. Since Seunig had made quite a name for himself as an outstanding rider and horseman, he was offered the job of Master of the Horse to the King of Yugoslavia. He accepted this offer under the condition that he first spend a year at the French military riding school in Saumur and after that half a year at the Royal Mews in London in order to learn the ceremonial and the protocol at the English Royal Court. After Seunig had organised the Royal Stables in Belgrade, he was granted a year to the Spanish Riding School in Vienna. At the end of the 1920s, the health of King Alexander deteriorated and he lost his interest in riding. The function of Master of the Horse diminished, and Seunig was offered the directorship of the newly founded military riding school. In 1933, when Seunig was up for promotion to become a general, he asked for his retirement. As a general, he would have been in command of a cavalry brigade; having no patriotic feelings for Yugoslavia, he did not think it appropriate to accept this command. After his retirement he kept riding, competing in several European countries, but he also started his literary career.

During the Second World War life for German-speaking people was very difficult in Slowenia, where he had settled in his ancestral mansion. The partisans burnt the house, so he fled to Germany . . . and entered the army. To those who criticise his second change of uniform, he had this to say: "The fact of my being German is not in the first place a mark of political conviction. It rather is a mark of human temperament and disposition; a special way to see things and to cope with them."

After the war Seunig travelled extensively, teaching and judging. In 1964 he came for the first time to the United States. In 1965 and in 1966 he was in Hawaii, California, the Midwest, British Columbia, Saskatchewan, Ontario and Vermont. A stroke in 1967 put an end to his travels.

His main work is *Von der Koppel bis zur Kapriole* (in English translation *Horsemanship*). A second book *Am Pulsschlag der Reitkunst* was published in English under the title *The Essence of Horsemanship* in 1983 (and reprinted in 1986).

Seunig had a style of writing seldom found in authors who write horse related books. He was poetic and picturesque, which often makes translation extremely difficult. Seunig's life was horses; his hobby was literature.

Simon of Athens

Born during the first quarter of the 5th century B C. Supposedly, he wrote the first book in the dialect of Attica. In this book he developed a system of equitation. The book is lost but for one chapter, dealing with the conformation of horses and the selection of them. We know about the contents of the whole book because Xenophon refers to it; so does Plinius the Elder, a Roman author. Savy de Lerville (*Von Olympia zum Olymp*) defends a thesis that Simon independently developed a system of horsemanship when he was assigned to resurrect a cavalry unit in Athens. For over a hundred years, there had been no cavalry in Athens; therefore, this unit had to be built up from scratch, and to do this in an organised way, Simon wrote what was to become the first cavalry manual, written around 450 B C. Since, according to the sources, Simon had a great reputation of being an excellent rider. Savy de Lerville points to the possibility that Simon's horses had been the models for the frieze of the

Parthenon. Against the theory that Xenophon had been involved with the sculptures, de Lerville stresses the fact that the frieze already existed when Xenophon was born.

Steinbrecht, Gustav (1808–85)

Son of a protestant minister, Steinbrecht was a veterinary student in Berlin when he started taking riding lessons from Louis Seeger, a pupil of the famous Oberbereiter in Vienna, Max von Weyrother. He married Seeger's niece and never left. He prepared horses for the circus, but contrary to Baucher, adhered strictly to classical principles. His posthumous book, *Das Gymnasium des Pferdes* goes directly back to la Guérinière and is still considered to be the fount of Germanic equitation.

Versailles, School of

In 1680, Louis XIV moved with his court to Versailles. The building of the palace, started during the reign of Louis XIII, had been completed. Since the court moved constantly through the country, a lot of horses were needed to move not only the king with his family but also hundreds of courtiers with their dependents. The men generally rode, while the women were driven in carriages. In 1682, the horses were moved to their new stables in Versailles. There were two, La Grande Écurie and La Petite Écurie, the big and the small stables. The big stable was for riding horses and the small stable for the king's horses, the carriage horses, hunters and post-horses. At one time, there were 4,000 horses in the big stables and 800 people were employed there. For the small stables the figures were about 60 riding horses and 300 coach horses, with 300 employees. In charge of all this was the "Grand Écuyer", generally called Monsieur le Grand. Since the 11th century those in charge of stables had gradually improved their status in the court hierarchy. When they had reached the summit and had become "Grand Écuyer", they had nobody above them but the king. The charge of the "Grand Écuyer", encompassed not only the royal stables, but also the royal stud-farm. He licensed those who taught in the riding academies, and he also was responsible for all the buying of the horses for the government. Both the Grande and the Petite Écurie were run by an "Écuyer Commandant", both of them assisted by several "écuyers ordinaires" and "écuyers cavalcadours". The last category were in charge of schooling the horses of the king and the princes.

The "Grand Écurie"

The place where the School of Versailles was born. The kings of France were always above average riders; some of them were passionate followers of hounds. And all had a great interest in artistic equitation. This interest made them spend large amounts of money to encourage this equitation. As a result, the riders could concentrate without any material worries on the development of this artistic equitation, which, because of the dedicated concentration of the most talented riders, became classical equitation. The same happened in Austria, where the "Spanische Hofreitschule" until 1918 belonged to the imperial court.

Xenophon (c. 430–c. 355 B C)

He was involved in the Pelopponesian war; after that, he joined Cyrus in his ill-fated campaigning against Artaxerxes. After the debacle, he led his 10,000 men through Asia Minor to the Black Sea. After more fighting in Thrace and Phrygia, he settled in 387 with his wife, a Greek from Asia Minor and his two sons in Scillonte, in the neighbourhood of Olympia. There he did most of his extensive writing. In this context, only his book about equitation and about the Cavalry commander are of interest. These books both have come to us intact. Therefore, it was presumed for a long time that Xenophon was the inventor of everything he describes, although he very often refers to Simon of Athens. Savy de Lerville has made it clear that we have to see Xenophon as the pupil and developer of Simon's ideas.

Bibliography

Albrecht, Kurt, *Dogmen der Reitkunst*. Orac-Pietsch, Wien, 1981.

Albrecht, Kurt, *Meilensteine auf dem Weg zur Hohen Schule*, Olms Presse, Hildesheim, 1983.

Albrecht, Kurt, *Dressurrichterfibel*. Orac-Pietsch, Wien, 1976.

Amman, Max, *Geschichte des Pferdesports*. Bucher, Luzern.

Anderson, J. K., *Ancient Greek Horsemanship*. University of California Press, Los Angeles, 1961.

d'Aure, Antoine Cartier, *Cours d'Équitation*. Émile Hazan, Paris, 1962.

Baucher, François, *Dictionnaire d'Équitation*. Émile Hazan, Paris, 1966.

Baucher, François, *Méthode d'Équitation*. Librairie de Mezière, Paris, 1976.

Baucher, François, *The Principles of Horsemanship*. Vinton & Co., London, 1919.

Beudant, Étienne, *Extérieure et Haute Ecole*. Charles Amat, Paris, 1923.

Blendinger, Wilhelm, *Menschen, Pferde und Kultur*. Paul Parey, Berlin, 1981.

Boisseau, Jeanne, *Notes sur l'enseignement de Nuno Oliveira*. Crépin-Leblon, Paris, 1979.

Boldt, Harry, *Das Dressur Pferd*. Edition Haberbeck, Lage-Lippe, 1978.

de Bragance, Diogo, *l'Equitation de la tradition française*. Odége, Paris, 1975.

Bürkner, Felix, *Ein Reiterleben*. Kornett Verlag, Verden-Aller, 1957.

Decarpentry, Albert, *Baucher et son école*. Lamarre, Paris, 1948.

Decarpentry, Albert, *Piaffer et Passage*, Oberthur, Rennes-Paris, 1932.

Decarpentry, Albert, *Équitation Académique*. Henri Neveu, Paris, 1949.

Decarpentry, Albert, *Academic Equitation*. J. A. Allen, London, 1971.

Challan Belval et Xavier Lesage, *Trois grands Écuyers de Manège de Saumur*.

Challan Belval, *Dressage*, Émile Hazan, Paris, 1964.

Chenevix-Trench, Charles, *A History of Horsemanship*, Longman, London, 1970.

Demko-Belansky, Tibor von, *So reitest Du*. Orac-Pietsch, Wien, 1973.

Dent, Anthony, *The Horse Through Fifty Centuries of Civilization*, Phaidon, London, 1974.

Dent, Anthony and Machin-Goodall, Daphne, *The Foals of Epona*. Galley Press, London, 1962.

Eisenberg, Baron von, *Die wohl eingerichtete Reitschule*. Olms Verlag, Hildesheim, 1974.

d'Endrödy, Agaston, *Give Your Horse a Chance*. J. A. Allen, London, 1959.

Faverot, de Kerbrech, *Dressage Méthodique*. Emile Hazan, Paris, 1958.

Fillis, James, *Journal de Dressage*. Flammarion, Paris, 1903.

v. Flotow and Rolf Becher, *Reitergedanken*. Sankt Georg, Berlin, 1938.

Frank, Oscar, *Reiten*. Schweizer Kavallerist, Pfäffikon, Zürich, 1970.

Frank and others. *Theoretisch gewuszt*. Schweizer Kavallerist Pfäffikon, Zürich, 1964.

French-Blake, Neil, *The World of Dressage*. Doubleday, New York, 1969.

Froissard, Jean, *Equitation*. Wilshire Book, Hollywood, 1972.

Fuchs, Karl Otto von, *Umgang mit Reittpferden* BLV, München, 1968.

Benoist-Gironière, Yves, *la Conquète du Cheval*. Champs Élysées, Paris, 1947.

Glahn, Erich, *Die Reitkunst am Scheideweg*. Erich Hoffmann, Heidenheim, 1956.

Glahn, Erich, *Die Weltreiterei und wir*.

Gogue, René, *Problèmes équestres*. Maloine, Paris, 1978.

Gordon, W. J., *The Horse World of London*, (1893). J. A. Allen, London.

Gossin, Danièle, *Psychologie et Comportement du cheval*. Maloine S.A., Paris, 1982.

Grisone, Federigo, *Gli Ordini di cavalcare*. Olms Presse, Hildesheim, 1972.

Gudin de Vallerin, Maurice, *Obstacle conduite et style*. Henri Neveu, Paris, 1950.

la Guérinière, François Robichon de, *École de Cavalerie*. Huart et Moreau, 1751.

Hançar, Franz, *Das Pferd in praehistorischer Zeit*. Herold, Wien, 1956.

Handler, Hans, *Die Spanische Hofreitschule*. Molder, Wien, 1972.

Harris, Charles, *Riding and Dressage*. Harris, London, 1981.

Hazslinszky, Geza von, *Dressuurryden, Protocol en Kritiek*. De Hoefslag den Haag.

Henriquet, Michel, À la Recherche de l'Équitation. Crépin-Leblond, Paris, 1968.

Henriquet, Michel, *Les Maîtres de l'Équitation classique*. André Gérard, Paris, 1974.

Herbermann, Erik F., Dressage Formula. J. A. Allen, London, 1978.

Heydebreck, Hans von, *Reitlehrer und Reiter*. Mittler und Sohn, Berlin, 1928.

Heydebreck, Hans von, *Das Gebrauchspferd*. Mittler und Sohn, Berlin, 1935.

Heydebreck, Hans von, *Die Deutsche Dressurprüfung*. Rudolf Georgi, Aachen, 1972.

Heyer, H. J., *Reflections on the Art of Horsemanship*. J. A. Allen, London, 1968.

l'Hotte, Alexis, *Officier de Cavalerie*. Émile Hazan, Paris, 1958.

l'Hotte, Alexis, *Questions Equestres*. Émile Hazan, Paris, 1960.

Hünersdorf, Ludwig, *Anleitung*. Olms Presse, Hildesheim, 1973.

Jankovich, Miklos, *Pferde, Reiter, Volkerstürme*. BLV, München.

Jonquère d'Oriola, Pierre, *A cheval sur cinq jolympiades*. Raoul Solar, 1968.

Joussaume, André, *Dressage*. Édition du fer à cheval, Paris, 1951.

Joussaume, André, *Progressive Dressage*. J. A. Allen, London, 1978.

Klimke, Reiner, *Military*. Franckh, Stuttgart, 1967.

Klimke, Reiner. *Grundausbildung des jungen Reitpferdes*. Franckh, Stuttgart, 1980.

Koch, Ludwig, *Die Reitkunst in Bilde*, 1925.

Kretschmar, Marit, *Pferd und Reiter im Orient*. Olms Presse, Hildesheim, 1980.

Kulesza, S. R., *Modern Riding*. Arco, New York, 1966.

Licart, Jean, *Comment apprendre à monter à Cheval*. J. Delmas et Cie, 1961.

Licart, Jean, *Basic Equitation*. J. A. Allen, London, 1968.

Loch, Sylvia, *The Royal Horse of Europe*. J. A. Allen, 1986.

Loon, Ernest van, *Ruiters en Rechters*. Zuidgroep, den Haag, 1978.

Machin-Goodall, Daphne, *Pferde der Welt*. Erich Hoffmann, Heidenheim, 1966.

Mairinger, Franz, *Horses are made to be Horses*, Rigby, Sydney, 1983.

Margot, *Comment juger*. Fédération française des sports équestres, Paris, 1967.

Markham, Gervase, *The Complete Horseman*. Houghton Mifflin, Boston, 1975.

Meagher, Jack, *Beating Muscle Injury in Horses*. Breakthrough, Briarcliff, N.Y., 1985.

Mennessier de la Lance, *Bibliographie Hippique*. Nieuwkoop de Graaf, 1971.

Monteilhet, André, *Les Maîtres de l'oeuvre équestre*. Odége, Paris, 1979.

Müseler, Wilhelm, *Reitlehre*. Paul Parey, Berlin.

Newcastle, William Cavendish, Duke of, *General System of Horsemanship*. de Hoefslag den Haag, 1973.

Newcastle, William Cavendish, Duke of, *Nouvelle Méthode* (de Solleysel). Olms Presse, Hildesheim, 1973.

Oeynhausen, Christian von, *Abrichtung*. Olms Presse, Hildesheim, 1977.

Oliveira, Nuno, *Haute École*. J. A. Allen, London, 1965.

Oliveira, Nuno, *Réflexions sur l'art équestre*. Crépin-Leblond, Paris, 1965.

Oliveira, Nuno, *Reflections on Equestrian Art*. J. A. Allen, London, 1976.

Oliveira, Nuno, *Classical Principles of the Art of Riding*. Howley & Russell.

Olstef, Sobène, *De l'équitation, la méthode et ses principes*. Crépin-Leblond, Paris, 1978.

d'Orgeix, Jean, *Équitation*. Robert Lafont, Paris, 1977.

Pluvinel, Antoine de, *le Manège royal*. J. A. Allen, London, 1970.

Pluvinel, Antoine de, *l'Instruction du Roy*. Griff, Paris, 1976.

Podhajsky, Alois, *Die Spanische Hofreitschule*. Hans Hammer, Wien, 1948.

Podhajsky, Alois, *Ein Leben fur die Lipizzaner*. Nymphenburger, München, 1960.

Podhajsky, Alois, *Die Klassische Reitkunst*. Nymphenburger, München, 1965.

Podhajsky, Alois, *Meine Lehrmeister die Pferde*. Nymphenburger, München, 1967.

Podhajsky, Alois, *Reiten und Richten*. Nymphenburger, München, 1973.

Rau, Gustav, *Die Reitkunst der Welt*. Sankt Georg, Düsseldorf, 1937.

Saint-Fort Paillard, Jean, *l'Équitation*. Chiron Sport, Paris, 1974.

Saint-Phalle, Jacques de, *Dressage et emploi du cheval de selle*. Crépin-Leblond, Paris, 1969.

Salins, Jean de, *Épaule en dedans*. Émile Hazan, Paris, 1957.

Santini, Piero, *Riding Reflexions. Country Life*, London, 1933.

Santini, Piero, *Caprilli Papers*. J. A. Allen, London, 1967.

Savy de Lerville, *Von Olympia zum Olymp*. Bengt Birck, München, 1972.

Saurel, Étienne, *Pratique de l'Équitation d'apres les Maîtres français*. Flammarion, 1964.

Saurel, Étienne, *Histoire de l'Équitation*. Stock, Paris, 1971.

Schäfer, Michael, *Wie werde ich Pferdekenner*. Nymphenburger, München, 1971.

Schäfer, Michael, *Die Sprache des Pferdes*. Nymphenburger, München, 1976.

Schäfer, Michael, *Andalusische Pferde*. Nymphenburger, Munchen, 1980.

Schäfer, Michael, *Mit Pferden leben*. Nymphenburger, München, 1982.

Schäfer, Michael, *Das Jahr des Pferdes*. Kynos, 1987.

Schusdziarra, H. & V., *Gymnasium des Reiters*. Paul Parey, Berlin, 1978.

Schusdziarra, H. & V., *Anatomy of Riding*. Breakthrough, Briarcliff, N.Y.

Seeger, Louis, *System der Reitkunst*. Olms Presse, Hildesheim, 1974.

Seherr-Thoss, H. von, *Dressurprüfungen*. M. & H. Schaper, 1967.

Seunig, Waldemar, *Von der Koppel bis zur Capriole*. Fritz und Wasmuth, Zürich, 1949.

Bibliography

Seunig, Waldemar, *Im Sattel zählte ich keine Zeit*. Sankt Georg, Düsseldorf, 1958.

Seunig, Waldemar, *Meister der Reitkunst*. Erich Hoffmann, Heidenheim, 1960.

Seunig, Waldemar, *Am Pulsschlag der Reitkunst*. Erich Hoffmann, Heidenheim, 1961.

Seunig, Waldemar, *Horsemanship*. Doubleday, New York, 1956.

Steinbrecht, Gustav, *Das Gymnasium des Pferdes*. Rudolf Georgi, Aachen, 1966.

Steinbrecht, Gustav, *Le Gymnase du Cheval*. Epiac, Paris, 1963.

Vigneron, Paul, *Le Cheval dans l'Antiquité*. Annales de l'Est, Nancy, 1968.

Waring, George H., *Horse Behavior*. Noyes Publications, 1983.

Wätjen, Richard, L. *Das Dressurreiten*. Paul Parey, Berlin, 1975.

Weyrother, Max Ritter von, *Hinterlassene Schriften*. Olms Presse, Hildesheim, 1977.

Wiesener (and others), *Die Kulturen de eurasischen Völker*. Athenaion, Frankfurt am Main, 1968.

Wiesener, Joseph, *Fahren und Reiten in Alteuropa und im alten Orient*. Olms Presse, Hildesheim, 1971.

Wynmalen, Henry, *Equitation*. Country Life, London, 1938.

Wynmalen, Henry, *Dressage*. Wilshire, Hollywood, 1972.

Xenophon, *Scripta Minora*. Harvard, Cambridge, 1968.

Zeuner, Frederick F. *Geschichte der Haustiere*. BLV, München, 1967.